A HISTORY OF
DISASTER

A HISTORY OF
DISASTER

Atlantic Canada's Worst Storms, Accidents, and Conflagrations

KEN SMITH

NIMBUS
PUBLISHING

Nimbus Publishing Limited
3731 Mackintosh St, Halifax, NS B3K 5A5
(902) 455-4286 nimbus.ca

Printed and bound in Canada

Printed and bound in Canada
Design: Reuben Hall
NB1164

Cover photo: St. John's, 1892
Library and Archives Canada Cataloguing in Publication

Smith, Ken, 1949 September 16-, author
A history of disaster : Atlantic Canada's worst storms, accidents, and conflagrations / Ken Smith.

First published in 2008.
Includes bibliographical references and index.
Issued in print and electronic formats.
ISBN 978-1-77108-175-7 (pbk.).— ISBN 978-1-77108-176-4 (html).—
ISBN 978-1-77108-177-1 (mobi)

1. Disasters—Atlantic Provinces—History. 2. Disasters—Atlantic Coast (Canada)—History. 3. Atlantic Provinces—History. I. Title.

FC2019.D58S65 2014   971.5   C2014-903210-2
                                                               C2014-903211-0

Nimbus Publishing acknowledges the financial support for its publishing activities from the Government of Canada through the Canada Book Fund (CBF) and the Canada Council for the Arts, and from the Province of Nova Scotia through Film & Creative Industries Nova Scotia. We are pleased to work in partnership with Film & Creative Industries Nova Scotia to develop and promote our creative industries for the benefit of all Nova Scotians.

For
Marina Lewis Smith

TABLE OF CONTENTS

ACKNOWLEDGEMENTS

I WOULD LIKE TO thank those who offered help and encouragement as the book progressed. To the staff of the New Brunswick, Nova Scotia, and Newfoundland archives, a special thank you for helping me find appropriate photos. I am also grateful for the guidance, advice, and encouragement offered by the editorial staff at Nimbus Publishing. And last, but never least, an enormous thank you to my wife, Verna, who encouraged me on this project from its inception.

INTRODUCTION

B Y WHAT CRITERIA are disasters measured? The number of lives lost is certainly one consideration, but perhaps just as important is the socio-economic damage resulting from a major unexpected tragedy. Ecological damage such as that incurred by the city of Halifax in 2003 at the hands of Hurricane Juan must also be considered. Throughout the city, scores of stately trees that had stood proudly for years were viciously uprooted and discarded. In another case, a fishing boat that sank in a storm lost all 150 on board. Is this a greater loss than a village that burns completely to the ground, wiping out the surrounding forest, along with the sawmills, docks, and ships, leaving hundreds homeless and destitute, but with a loss of only ten souls? In other cases, the news media can sometimes add fame or notoriety to what might otherwise be considered a minor tragedy. Because it received an unprecedented amount of radio coverage, the 1936 Moose River gold mine disaster is still remembered today in word and song as one of Canada's most famous disasters, even though only three men were involved and only one died. In such cases disasters live on as legend, the high drama, heroism, and epic struggles for survival heightened with each telling.

This book tells the stories of forty-three disasters that struck Atlantic Canada from the eighteenth century to the present day. I have included mostly those disasters that resulted in at least twenty deaths, although all the factors mentioned above—emotional impact, rescue efforts, news coverage, and social and cultural influence—were also factors in these selections. As too many of these events have been largely forgotten, it is my fervent wish that this book serve as a brief history lesson, opening a window onto past events and offering a true understanding of humanity's character.

St. John's in ruins following the Great Fire, 1892

Natural disasters are older than humankind itself. As long as our ever-changing planet spews forth fiery volcanoes, spawns great ocean storms and deadly tsunamis, and shifts our terra firma with massive earthquakes, humanity will forever be at risk of suffering a natural catastrophe. For a long time, Aboriginal peoples of the region faced natural disaster in the form of fires, droughts, floods, and storms, often investing these events with spiritual importance.

For generations, stories have been passed down by word of mouth and through song, many becoming legend in the process. With technological progress, we thought we could control, predict, or at least be forewarned of these tempestuous outbreaks of nature. But we could not—at least not all of the time.

There have been well over three hundred events documented as major disasters in Canada to the present day. The land, air, and waters surrounding Atlantic Canada account for nearly one-third of these tragic events, mainly because the Atlantic region was settled and populated long before any explorers arrived in central and western Canada. Most of the disasters in those early days were natural, such as the great ocean storms that devastated scores of sailing ships, from tiny fishing-fleet schooners to huge ocean-going clippers. But as the region's towns and cities grew and prospered, and its industries and technologies flourished, human-caused disasters became more common.

Nova Scotia's coal mining industry, for example, saw several disasters during the nineteenth and twentieth centuries. The great mines of Cape Breton, Pictou, and Cumberland counties employed thousands of men, and sometimes even children. The livelihood of these workers—and indeed the economy of their communities—depended totally on the production of coal. Working conditions in the deep collieries were often deadly. Methane gas, carbon monoxide, and coal dust were just waiting for the slightest spark to trigger a disastrous explosion. Ground movements, called bumps, also took the lives of scores of miners. These disasters knew no bounds and often towns had to close permanently, leaving only destitution, depression, and a shattered economy.

Air travel, perhaps one of the most significant technological advances of the past century, has not escaped disaster. Over the past fifty years, several accidents involving airplanes, both civilian and military, have been responsible for the deaths of hundreds of travellers in Atlantic Canada. One crash alone, 1998's Swissair disaster, left 229 dead.

It is not without reason that the rest of Canada has tended to look (not without fondness) upon Atlantic Canadians as a breed apart, especially upon those who earn their livelihood on the sea. In many ways, disaster and the constant threat of tragedy have shaped Atlantic Canadians' lives and defined their culture. But while the positive aspects of humanity shone through in many of these events, the bravery, compassion, and heroic rescue efforts of those involved are what, in a twist of irony, make these events even more tragic.

PART ONE
Pre-1900

P RIOR TO THE British-French conflict of the mid-1700s, Atlantic Canada was populated by the Mi'kmaq and Maliseet, along with a growing Acadian population. In English-held Newfoundland, settlers were already taking advantage of the teeming abundance of fish in the coastal waters. In these formative years no large-scale industries had yet developed in the region. Villages were scattered and remote, only accessible by rough wagon track or small boat. Plagued by the harsh Atlantic winters, drought, forest fire, raging gales, and outbreaks of lethal epidemics, early settlers had no choice but to adapt. Most of these earliest disasters went unrecorded, but were passed down through folk history.

The British victory in the Seven Years' War resulted in an influx of settlers to the Atlantic region. Twenty years later, Loyalists from New England added to the growing population of Nova Scotia, New Brunswick, and Prince Edward Island. Villages began cropping up throughout the region. Saint John, Fredericton, Halifax, and St. John's were developing into cities of major importance as the abundant timber resources fed the growing lumber and shipbuilding industries. The Nova Scotia and Newfoundland fisheries thrived as new lucrative markets were found. The huge coalfields in eastern Nova Scotia developed rapidly as the region entered the age of steam-driven machinery. As the population increased, fishing fleets grew and mining towns expanded.

With this increased industry came disasters. A monstrous forest fire destroyed the village of Newcastle, New Brunswick, in 1825. A few years later both Fredericton and St. John's were almost completely destroyed by fire. Before the nineteenth century was out, Saint John would suffer a similar fate. The Yankee Gale of 1851 and the Saxby Gale of 1869 became infamous for the appalling level of death and destruction wreaked upon land and sea alike. The bitter cold of the winter seasons showed no mercy in ravaging sealing fleets in Newfoundland. In Nova Scotia the inherent dangers of coal mines were evident as a tragic methane blast in 1891 claimed 125 miners. But the fishermen, the miners, and the lumbermen, most of whom knew no other way of life, accepted the danger, the risks, and the heartbreak of loss. Strong and close bonds developed between their fellow workers, their families, and their neighbours. Moral, cultural, and spiritual integrity kept the communities close, and despite the risks, life was considered good.

1758 THE *VIOLET* AND THE *DUKE WILLIAM* PERISH ON THE HIGH SEAS

In 1755 the great upheaval of the Acadians began. Known to the Acadians themselves as *le Grand Dérangement*, this dispersal, or deportation, was the darkest period in the history of this proud people. Thousands of farmers and fisherfolk in Nova Scotia (which included New Brunswick at the time) were violently and cruelly torn from their homes and families and thrust onto waiting ships to be taken to a scattering of places, including New England, the Caribbean, Louisiana, and France. Not all Acadians lived in Nova Scotia at the time: many had moved earlier to the French-held Île Saint-Jean (present-day Prince Edward Island), and many others joined them after escaping the initial deportation in 1755. The Acadians prospered on the fertile island soil. Farming and fishing were good, and the Acadians were able to supply Louisbourg, the huge guardian fortress on Cape Breton Island, then known as Île

Challenging the mighty Atlantic Ocean

Royale, with fresh meat, fish, and produce. The French felt safe on Île Saint-Jean because England was not at war with France, at least not yet.

That was about to change when, in 1756, the Seven Years' War began. By 1758 most of the Acadians in Nova Scotia had been rounded up and deported, Louisbourg had fallen to the English, and the Acadian inhabitants on Île Saint-Jean, now left without protection, were at the mercy of the British. The order to begin deporting the Acadians from the island came in the fall of 1758. Nine troopships, most of which had been used to transport the British army from Britain for the capture of Louisbourg, were ordered to begin loading deportees, who would be sent to France. Several of the ships' captains complained bitterly that it was much too late in the year to attempt an Atlantic crossing. Captain Nichols of the *Duke William*, which was the largest ship in the fleet, protested vehemently that his ship needed major refitting and was not seaworthy enough to take on a fall crossing. His words fell on deaf ears, and Nichols was ordered to carry out his duties at once.

Thus, on September 8, 1758, several thousand Acadians of Île Saint-Jean were captured, rounded up, and forced at gunpoint on to the nine waiting ships. Their farms, homes, and possessions left behind were immediately burnt and destroyed by the British troops. For more than two months, the flotilla lingered in the Canso Strait area, waiting for a strong wind to sail on. On November 25, a strong northwest gale blew in and the flotilla was underway, albeit at the most dangerous and treacherous time of the year to be on the open seas. A few days later, the fleet ran into a ferocious storm, the sea running so high that the ships could not keep together. The fleet soon dispersed in the raging sea. Somehow the *Duke William* and the *Violet* came across each other a couple of weeks later, again in storm conditions.

The *Violet* was in a desperate condition and leaking badly, unable to withstand much more battering from the raging ocean. All its pumps were either broken or plugged, and Captain Sugget feared the worst. The *Duke William* was having its own problems taking on water and couldn't supply any pumps to the *Violet*. A particularly strong squall came up quickly and the two ships lost visibility. When it cleared, the *Violet* was nowhere to be seen. Sadly, it had gone down, taking all hands and four hundred Acadians with it.

While it was all over for the *Violet*, the *Duke William* was struggling valiantly to stay afloat. Captain Nichols ordered all on board, including prisoners, to man the pumps and bailers. For almost four days they desperately pumped, bailed, and plugged the massive leaks on the ship, but more water came in than was going out. By the fourth day, Captain Nichols knew they were fighting a losing battle, and ordered the two lifeboats out. Since the lifeboats were to be for the crew of thirty-six, the pastor of the Acadian prisoners was asked to speak with his people, give absolution, and ask them to prepare for eternity. The good pastor did this, then, on seeing the longboats being launched, jumped over the ship's rails and found himself a seat, abandoning his flock to their fate. Luckily four of the Acadians found a small jolly boat and they quickly piled in. The lifeboats were hardly gone from the doomed *Duke William* when a deep rumble was heard from within the ship. A moment later the ship went down, drowning three hundred Acadian prisoners. The longboats and the jolly boat all eventually reached the shores of England safely. Of the other seven ships taking part in the deportation, it was assumed that at least six reached the shores of France. The seventh, the *Ruby*, was also lost, and 200 of the 310 Acadians on board perished in the Atlantic. (Unlike the *Violet* and *Duke William*, little is known of the circumstances surrounding the *Ruby*'s sinking.)

The sinking of the *Violet* and *Duke William*, one of the earliest recorded Atlantic Canadian disasters, was also one of the most deadly. The seven hundred Acadians who perished were not hard-edged, experienced sailors who chose a seafaring life. They were innocent men, women, and children who asked for nothing except to be left in peace. Instead, they were caught between two warring nations and paid a bitter price.

1825 THE MIRAMICHI IN FLAMES

PROSPERITY

In 1825 the tiny pioneer village of Newcastle was a thriving community located just upriver from the great Miramichi estuary. Newcastle and its adjacent settlements were comfortably strung along the banks of the mighty river, with homes sometimes being built right up to the riverbanks. Natural fields were at a premium because the great pine, fir, and spruce forests grew right up to the settlers' backyards, almost completely locking the villages to the river. Cleared homestead acreages were in many cases quite small, having been cut, cleared, and burned from the surrounding woodland. As an industry, farming was mostly overshadowed by the numerous forestry, lumbering, and shipbuilding enterprises. In fact, a great majority of the men of the region worked in sawmills, shipyards, or as woodworkers in the deep forests along the banks of the upper Miramichi. Although fishermen were also doing a healthy trade in 1825, the main export trade came from the forestry industry, despite the fact that England was experiencing an economic depression during this period and a decreased demand for timber was forcing prices down.

The hard-working population consisted mainly of Loyalist settlers who relied on the forestry harvest of mast and shipbuilding timber, as well as on the bountiful sea catches. Some twelve years earlier, the Gilmour and Rankin firm of shipbuilders had set up shop in the Douglastown area, where Alexander Rankin quickly built his lumberyard into a highly successful and profitable operation. The young lumber baron and shipbuilder was well liked and thoroughly respected throughout the string of small Miramichi communities. It was his fair, honest, and hard-working attitude that led him and his firm to become the mainstay of the area's economy by 1825. The disaster that occurred that year was to shake the Rankin establishment to the core, but the resourceful and resilient young businessman was back on his feet and on the build within three years.

In 1825 the Miramichi area was just recovering from a small outbreak of typhoid fever, not an unusual occurrence for a pioneer village. The people of the small village of Newcastle were undeterred, however, as there was still work and prosperity for all.

DROUGHT

The summer of 1825 was warm, but not unusually so. Planting was early and there was every reason to expect that the fall harvest would be one of the best ever. Then the summer rains stopped, and temperatures rose. By the beginning of October, the fall rains had not yet arrived and the word "drought" was on the lips of many. Aside from a brief sprinkle one afternoon in September, there had not been any precipitation for ten straight weeks. But there was heat—and plenty of it. Steady daily temperatures over ninety degrees Fahrenheit soon parched the land. Grass turned sickly brown and wells and waterholes dried up. Sandbars were showing up at numerous places along the river as the water levels dropped drastically. Small streams became gravel beds, and the local marshes were now just fields of dried, cracked mud. Potatoes were turning brown in the fields and grass and flowers crunched underfoot, as did the smallest of twigs along forest trails. Much of the fall garden harvest was shrivelled and undersized. The lack of wind or any kind of air movement made the hot air stifling.

WARNINGS

By October 6 the situation had not improved. The smell of wood-smoke hung in the heavy, still air, the wilting leaves on the trees hardly moving for lack of even a gentle breeze. The dead heat and tremendous lassitude were more worrisome to the village folk than the threat of fire. Despite rumours, reports, and warnings from several sources about the rapidly escalating danger of a catastrophic fire, the people of Miramichi were generally unconcerned as there was no imminent danger to the village. But woodcutters and lumbermen were returning home; too hot and too dangerous, they said. One little spark from someone out having an evening pipe would be all that was needed to start a fire in the tinder-dry land. The Aboriginal people, it was reported, were also leaving the woods, heading for the banks of the Miramichi. Moose, deer, and many other small animals were making their way to the safety of larger lakes and riverbanks, some more than forty miles away. At night the glow of several fires could be seen, but the townsfolk assumed the danger was far away and in a different direction. One exception was old Grandmère Bubier, who claimed to have a "second sight." She urged her reluctant family to dig a deep "potato hole"—and her insistence would save many lives.

INFERNO

The morning of October 7 dawned hot and heavy. An ever-thickening haze of pungent woodsmoke held over the village. Smoke could also be seen rising from the forests to the west and north. James Wright, an elderly woodsman and former soldier, went through the village of Newcastle frantically beating his drum and urging the people to flee the approaching flames. Most just smiled indulgently at the old man and went about their business. What the village

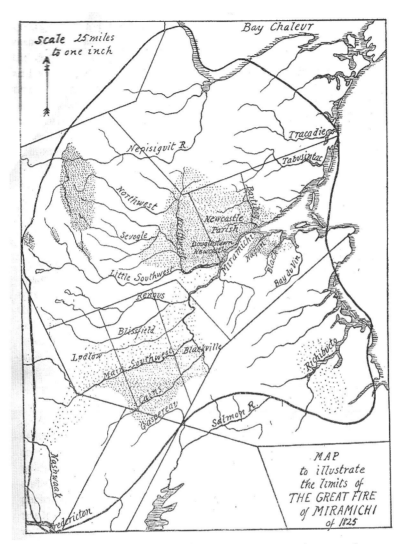

A map showing the extent of the Great Miramichi Fire of 1825

folk did not realize was that a series of large fires were rapidly join-ing together into a gigantic front, and the wind was turning from the south to a southeasterly direction. Ripping along the heavily forested banks of the Miramichi River, the rapidly approaching inferno was heading straight for Douglastown and Newcastle. A terrible tragedy was about to unfold. As the sun—by now a pale orange disc overshadowed by a looming smoky darkness—finally set, the people of Newcastle were casting wary eyes at the skies and listening intently to the crashing and booming noises coming nearer and nearer to the village.

Around 8:00 PM, an intense wall of flame appeared over the unsuspecting village, poised like a fiery predator. The leading wall of the fire was destroying everything in its path while consuming oxygen at such a rate that the resulting vacuum caused hurricane-force winds at its front. Trees ignited instantly. Dry deadwood was exploding and flaming embers were swirling among the wind and heavy smoke, landing on homes and businesses, as well as on several ships moored on the river. Within minutes, most of the buildings in the village were aflame. In some cases, flying cinders even jumped across the river and set off ravaging fires in the tiny community of Napan.

Pandemonium, fear, and confusion reigned. Death came rapidly to many who, caught unaware and asleep in their beds, became trapped by the flames. Others attempted to leap from roofs and windows and were struck by flaming debris swirling about in the deadly maelstrom of fire and smoke. Many of the town's recovering typhoid victims, still weak, perished in their beds. Most people ran for the safety of the great river, grabbing and hanging on to anything that could keep them afloat. Sadly, at least ten were overcome by river currents and drowned. In the confusion, some of the panicked villagers ran the wrong way, toward the woods, and were quickly devoured by the flames. Many burst into flames as they ran, while others simply dropped to their knees in wide-eyed terror and prayed, believing that the end of the world had come.

The last remaining house in Newcastle, 1890

Whole families perished, including one family of nine and one of seven. Many suffocated in the streets. One man jumped into his well with several others. All perished. One greedy father left his children at home so he could loot now-abandoned businesses. When he returned, all his children were dead. Several ships at anchor caught fire and burned at their moorings as red-hot cinders rained down on the decks. Wild animals, including a black bear, were huddled neck deep in the river, nestled among the cattle and terror-stricken villagers. Grandmère Bubier hustled all her family and several others down into the "potato hole" her sons had so reluctantly dug, covered the top with boards and gravel, and hunkered down to wait out the inferno. The fire levelled the village in three hours, and the crashing, howling winds could be heard all night. Breathing was difficult in the potato hole, but all eleven family members survived the ordeal, including the family dog. By morning the winds had died as it grew cooler and a fog set in. It was all over.

The extent of the Great Fire was becoming clear as reports came in. The communities of Moorfield, Black River, and Napan were destroyed. Douglastown, directly in the fire's path, was wiped out, with all but six of the village's seventy buildings destroyed. Newcastle was also hit extremely hard, with only 12 of 260 buildings left standing. At least 160 people in the Newcastle-Douglastown area and up to 200 in the surrounding settlements lost their lives and many more remained unaccounted for. Three to four hundred were badly burned and more than two thousand were left homeless and destitute. Three large vessels burnt. Among livestock, 375 head of cattle and hundreds of sheep were lost. The fire burnt approximately five thousand square miles, fully one-fifth of the province of New Brunswick, although there were in fact several large but separate fires within this area. Many settlements in the upper branches of the Miramichi were also completely destroyed.

THE AFTERMATH

The lieutenant-governor of New Brunswick, Sir Howard Douglas, newly appointed in 1824 and already well liked throughout the province, visited the areas worst affected by the fire a few days later, travelling between Fredericton and Newcastle. Small homesteads and hamlets lay smouldering and blackened all the way from Nashwaaksis and along the Miramichi Valley, but the pitiful scene that the lieutenant-governor encountered at Newcastle was one of the most appalling in its level of destruction and heartbreaking devastation. Douglas immediately ordered relief supplies to the destitute survivors. One thousand barrels of flour, five hundred barrels of pork, and almost two thousand British pounds worth of clothes were purchased at once, much of the expense coming out of Douglas's own purse. Then he immediately sent wagons to Quebec to purchase, on New Brunswick Treasury notes, a larger quantity of food and clothing. It was clear that without immediate relief, the devastated and homeless villagers would be extremely hard-pressed to survive a frigid New Brunswick winter. Word soon came from England that because the country was in the midst of an economic depression, relief funds were unavailable. Fortunately, as a result of a desperate appeal that went out to the citizens of England and its colonies, over forty thousand British pounds were collected, which greatly assisted those who had lost everything in the fire.

Economically, the area was devastated. Much of the large pine forest that supported the area's masting industry was wiped out. The Miramichi area had been responsible for over half of the province's exports, and it would take several years before the timber trade was healthy once again. The disaster, though unparalleled in size, also left some unburned tracts of forest, and the new growths of juniper would eventually serve the shipbuilding trade well. Though much of the forestry industry had to be shifted to the northern and western areas of the province, enough timber was left standing to keep the area alive economically, though it would take a few years to rebuild. In a rare case of good fortune, or perhaps providence, the home- and shipbuilding operations of the Rankin family, so crucial to the region's economic health, had been spared complete destruction.

The people of the Miramichi were nothing if not resilient, and with the determination, hard work, and guidance of the Alexander Rankin Company, the area was back on its feet within three years, and looking forward to a bright future as the forest slowly grew back.

1846 FIRE DESTROYS ST. JOHN'S

St. John's, Newfoundland, is no stranger to fire, but the conflagration of 1846 was especially disastrous if measured by the number of homes burnt and people left homeless. On George Street, one of the most populated and congested areas in the heart of the city, a cabinetmaker's pot of glue left to warm on a hot stove suddenly ignited, spewing flaming glue everywhere. The building was quickly lost to the rapidly growing flames, which within a few moments had spread to surrounding apartment buildings. The fire alarm sounded, but firefighting equipment was still rudimentary and no water was readily available. Little could be done.

The inferno, fuelled by fresh winds, reached Queen Street, and then Water Street, before spreading in different directions. Firebreaks failed to stop the flames even though more homes were dynamited to create space. All to no avail, as the dynamite just filled the air with flaming debris that spun off in all directions, creating new fires. All firefighting efforts were in vain, and the

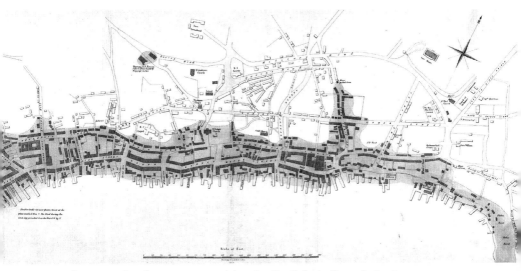

A map showing the damage caused by the St. John's fire of 1846

inferno went on to consume everything along Duckworth Street, King's Road, and the harbourfront. Many citizens scrambled wildly to save whatever they could of their belongings. Most of the larger buildings, some built of stone and brick, were devoured by the flames. Government offices, schools, churches, and many large commercial stores were likewise destroyed. In all, over two thousand buildings were lost to the great fire. The twelve thousand people who lost their homes and most of their possessions represented 57 per cent of the city's population.

Less than two hundred thousand pounds were recovered from a total insurance claim of almost a million pounds. It must surely be considered fortunate that only five lives were lost as a result of such a terrible fire. Relief efforts began the next day when money poured in from other towns and various government agencies. Officials drew up rebuilding plans, with major building changes in the burnt-out district. All new buildings were to be of stone construction, streets were to be widened, fireproof materials were to be used, and older wooden homes that had survived the blaze were to be removed. Within a few years St. John's would rebound; little did they realize that another huge conflagration in 1892 would nearly destroy the city in a horrendous outbreak.

1850 FREDERICTON BURNS TO THE GROUND

Many of the major towns and cities of Atlantic Canada can list at least one catastrophic fire in their chronicle of historical events. While certainly disastrous, fires involving the loss of a few blocks of buildings were not at all uncommon. But in a few instances, fires destroyed most of the town or city. This was the case in Fredericton, New Brunswick, in 1850. In that year the town experienced a blaze so ferocious that most of the downtown area was reduced to smoking ruins within twelve hours. Citizens in the thriving capital woke up to a bright and sunny Monday morning on November 10, little realizing that by the evening more than two thousand stunned and desolate victims, many with only the clothes on their backs, would be frantically searching for shelter from the cold autumn night. Over 1,550 homes were lost to one of the greatest conflagrations in New Brunswick history.

Like so many fires in those days, it started from a simple act of carelessness—in this case, an errant spark from an improperly lit pipe. The story begins on an early Monday afternoon at the Carleton Street schoolhouse, where several men were employed by

Miss McLaughlin, the local schoolmistress, to saw firewood for the coming winter. Working steadily all morning, the men stopped for lunch before resuming their sawing. At around 1:30 PM, one of the workmen paused for a quick smoke. Although it was a warm and sunny day, the wind was quite brisk. As the man attempted to light up, a gust of wind blew a few sparks from his pipe to the dry sawdust in the woodshed. Perhaps the workmen did not see the spark land and the fire catch, for in a few moments the woodshed was ablaze and soon the schoolhouse caught fire. From there, the flames, fanned by the fresh wind, jumped to the adjacent Methodist Church. The fire department was quickly called in but proved useless. In 1850 steam-driven pumps had not yet arrived, and the tiny hand-worked pumps in use were inadequate. Worst of all, the pumps had no capacity for storing water, and there was no water close by.

The area between King and Queen streets was now afire, with the flames jumping rapidly as the oxygen burned, increasing the wind at the fire's forefront. Everyone pitched in; citizens and militia alike formed bucket brigades to try to at least slow down the blaze. An hour or so after the fire began, it was becoming quite clear that the battle was lost and a catastrophic disaster was in the making. The air was acrid with smoke as flaming cinders flew everywhere, landing on buildings in every direction. Families desperately hauled their furniture and possessions into the street to prevent burning. It was in vain, as the inferno consumed everything in its path. Men tried throwing water on their rooftops, hoping to save their homes, but such acts were useless, and home after home went up in smoke. Queen Street, a main business district, was decimated. Stores and warehouses alike were quickly destroyed, along with valuable winter stock. Out of three hundred buildings in a four-block area bounded by Carleton, Brunswick, Queen, and St. John streets, all but four were destroyed. Eighteen acres of the city were burned.

Compounding the fire's destruction were the dregs of humanity, the thieves and shoplifters, who soon went about their business. There was no established police force in those days and the militia was busy fighting the fire. One brazen thief pilfered a keg of gunpowder, shouldered it, and proceeded to run straight up the street, fires raging on both sides and sparks and cinders flying. (Onlookers probably hoped the keg would blow, but the nonplussed thief managed to get away to safety.)

Many citizens lost all their possessions when their homes burnt. In most cases their place of work was also gone. Destitute families had no food and no shelter. The city council acted decisively, immediately ordering that tents and shelters be set up in Officers' Square for the homeless. Surrounding communities gladly supplied clothing, food, and temporary shelter to those displaced. It took a few months, but eventually rebuilding started, people found jobs, and the economy was soon rebounding. Many of the destroyed buildings were small wooden structures packed closely together. The rebuilding resulted in larger, better-built homes, many of stone and with larger lots. Roadways and sidewalks were widened. Street lighting was improved with the introduction of gaslights, and soon railroad and telegraph service was available. Disastrous as the Great Fire of 1850 may have been, it did not deter Fredericton from moving forward to a greater and prosperous future.

1851 THE YANKEE GALE SMASHES THE NEW ENGLAND FLEET

Prince Edward Island has always had a proud and vibrant fishing industry. In the mid-nineteenth century, the usually placid waters surrounding this lovely island were teeming with fish of all species, especially mackerel. Harvests were good and fishing schooners from Nova Scotia, New Brunswick, and Newfoundland all headed for this favoured fishing ground each fall. Even more numerous were ships from the New England fleet.

Hundreds of boats from Boston, Portland, Gloucester, and several other American ports were fishing the waters of northeast PEI on October 3, 1851. The day started out as an ordinary and quite pleasant one. Although the sky was overcast, the air was warm and the winds calm. As sunset arrived, the sky took on something of a glassy appearance. Old sailors looked at this as a harbinger of extremely bad weather. They were right. That Friday evening a storm roared in from the northeast and lasted for two days. Although it affected only a small area of the PEI coast, the storm is remembered by many as perhaps the most damaging in Island history. The New England fishing fleet, caught just offshore, suffered devastating losses: several hundred ships were wrecked and scores of fishermen lost. Many of those lost were closely related; in one case, a Captain James Wixon lost four of his sons in the storm. In the aftermath, the northeast shores of the Island were littered with wreckage, much of which would remain for well over a half century as morbid testimony to the ferocity of what was named the Yankee Gale of 1851.

Most of the ships caught in the Yankee Gale were schooners. Even many of those that made it safely to shore suffered terrible damage. The storm split mainsails, toppled masts, and tangled rigging into heaps; it swept the decks relentlessly and most of the valuable cargo of fish, stored in barrels on deck, was washed away, along with ropes, equipment, hatch covers, and, in many cases, crewmembers. Those who were fortunate enough to make it to shore were cold, exhausted, and barely alive. Islanders living in the numerous villages along the coast flocked to the seashore as boats were spotted. Opening their homes and hearts, Islanders showed the true meaning of compassion and kindness, taking the unfortunate fishermen into their own warm homes, feeding them, and taking care of all their needs until they were able to go on. For several days rumours were rampant as to which ships were lost and which made it safely to port. Vessels reported as lost with all hands were seen in port, while others reported as saved were never seen again, nor were their crews. Many bodies floated to shore or were found inside wreckage, and many of the dead were aboard ships that were able to limp into port.

Many claimed the poor design of the American boats was a major cause of much of the loss and damage. The *Islander* reported that many of the American captains panicked and headed their ships—many unlighted—headlong for the nearest port in blinding conditions and in unknown waters.

One of the few Canadian ships did it the right way. A Captain Bell, instead of rushing to shore when the gale began, kept at sea until daybreak. When he had enough light to see, he headed for New London, but found it too hazy to attempt a run in. So he changed course and headed for North Cape instead, rounding the point and making for West Point. He lay in lee, the water calm as a puddle, until the storm eased up. If others had taken similar actions, many lives and ships would have been saved.

A Grand Banks fishing schooner

Although many of the fishing boats were insured, total losses were staggering. Along with severe damage to most of the three hundred or so surviving boats, hundreds of barrels of fish were lost. The final tally of lives lost was in the hundreds, leaving countless widows and fatherless children.

Though PEI, being a small island, has not known as many disastrous events as the neighbouring provinces, the Yankee Gale of 1851 has to rank among the most infamous of all Maritime sea disasters.

1869 THE SAXBY GALE ARRIVES ON SCHEDULE

THE PREDICTION

Imagine a storm so powerful, so intense, and so destructive that stories of its ferocity have reached legendary status and are still being passed down today. During any of the wild October gales that are common along the Fundy tidal region of New Brunswick, one can still hear the retelling of the great Saxby Gale of 1869, perhaps on some black and rain-swept night while gathered round a cozy cottage fireplace, safe from the shrieking winds and thundering waves. So where did the name Saxby come from? Back in those days, hurricanes, gales, and tropical storms were not given names as they are today. Was Saxby the name of a place, a person, or a thing?

The true story goes something like this. In 1868 the British Royal Navy had the honour of having under its command a young lieutenant who went by the name of Stephen Martin Saxby. Now, undoubtedly young Saxby, being an engineering instructor, was a competent officer and fine young man. He just happened to have, as many young men do, a secondary interest—a hobby, if you will. Saxby happened to be fascinated by astronomy, especially as it related to weather patterns. In late 1868 Saxby, after having studied his observations carefully, came to some startling conclusions. It was his firm belief that the position of the moon in relation to the Earth and other celestial bodies could affect the weather greatly, tides in particular, and to such a degree that he could actually predict a major gale (or hurricane) far in advance, even up to the exact day. In 1863 he had predicted, with some degree of accuracy, lunar-caused weather changes in parts of England, gaining a few believers.

In December 1868 Saxby wrote a letter to a London newspaper warning that, because of the position of the moon in relation to the Earth and the magnetic influence of the lunar cycle on the tides, an extremely destructive gale would occur, along with extraordinarily high water levels along coastal areas. The confident Mr. Saxby even went out on a limb and predicted the date, October 5, 1869, but did not go so far as to foretell exactly where the devastation would occur. Saxby's warnings were read widely in papers in both the United States and Canada, including the Fundy region. Many scoffed at the young man's prediction, saying that October was a common month for gales, so a storm occurring near the date mentioned would not be so unusual. But most just ignored the warnings, dismissing Saxby as something of a charlatan and an attention seeker.

THE STORM

On October 4, 1869, a storm *did* strike, hitting the Fundy region so hard over two days that it was considered the most intense and destructive gale ever recorded up to that date. Young Saxby surely must have been gloating just a tad. But was the date truly prophetic, or, as most people (but not all) believed, just an eerie coincidence? Many people living in the area where the storm struck were not even aware of Saxby's prediction until after the gale had passed. The unusual storm could easily be explained by professional weather observers who noted that tides were extraordinarily high that month due to the moon's gravitational pull. That was normal. On October 4, it was noted, an extremely large band of rainstorms was moving in from the western regions and heading directly for the Saint John area. At the same time, a large tropical storm was being tracked from its origins in the Caribbean, up the Gulf Stream,

The paddlewheeler New York, *1869*

and along the eastern seaboard toward southern New Brunswick. The storm, nearing hurricane strength, was on a collision course with the huge front moving in from the east. In the early evening of October 4, the two forces merged, combining with the above normal tides, forming a whopper of a gale—a perfect storm, as we would say today.

The day started out as a perfectly pleasant fall day. The sun rose, burning off the morning mist, and the day promised to be warm and sunny. All along the Bay of Fundy, the winds were light, the sea gentle. If ever the expression "calm before the storm" was appropriate, it was on October 4, 1869. In the late morning, subtle changes began to occur. A slight increase in the breeze began to whip up whitecaps in the bays along the coast. The heat started to become damp and sultry. A few hours later, the wind picked up considerably and the surf began to roar. On the horizon, dark, leaden clouds loomed as the sky began to darken ominously with the increasing wind. By late afternoon, the storm had reached hurricane force and was ripping branches from trees; it soon advanced to tearing up the trees themselves. A few hours later, roofs were being ripped off homes and barns as the Saxby Gale unleashed its terrible fury.

DAMAGE

From Eastport, Maine, through the islands of Grand Manan and Campobello, and up through the lowland regions of the Bay of Fundy, the raging gale wrought a path of destruction and death. Terrified people in tiny villages and farms huddled together in basements and storm cellars, completely cut off from neighbours, waiting the storm out in abject fear and uncertainty as the shrieking wind tore roofs off houses, barns, and outbuildings alike. Uprooted trees came crashing down everywhere as winds of ninety miles an hour roared through, in some places accompanied by twelve inches of rain. The damage done by tides much higher than anyone at the time had ever seen was appalling—it was as though a huge tidal wave had rushed into the Bay of Fundy. Dykes that had stood for more than a century overflowed and broke open. At Grand Pré, Tantramar, Petitcodiac, Falmouth, and other places, cattle and livestock were washed away, along with hay, harvesting equipment, fishing gear, lobster traps, barns, and sometimes human beings.

A locomotive in St. Stephen, 1869

Along the coastline, hundreds of boats were completely destroyed at their moorings or washed inland to be smashed against rocks and trees.

At St. Andrews alone, 123 vessels were washed up onto the beach. At Lepreau, tragedy struck when a boat, the *Genii*, was lost with eleven men aboard. In some cases whole families were flooded and swept from their homes. Four children died as they desperately tried to hang on to floating debris with the rest of their family.

Houses were lifted off their foundations and floated out to sea. One young couple tried to make it across a flooding marsh with their horse and buggy. Both horse and buggy were swept away, and the young girl was lost. The young man barely managed to survive. Hundreds of similar stories abounded among those who witnessed the savage gale. While many told of fear, confusion, and sheer terror, others describe acts of bravery and heroism and raw courage. Such was the great Saxby Gale. While the total number of lives lost to the storm may be unknown, it is assumed scores, perhaps even hundreds, fell victim to the savage two-day fury. Although the Saxby Gale is best known for the man who predicted it, the magnitude of the damage cause by this true "storm of the century" would be enough to make it legendary.

1873 RMS *ATLANTIC* SINKS NEAR HALIFAX

The industrialization of the second half of the nineteenth century brought great changes in many spheres, especially in transportation and travel. Puffing great billows of steam and smoke, newly built railway locomotives were opening new lands and territories throughout the world. People were travelling across the seas more than ever before, especially on the new breed of ocean liners introduced by the White Star Line, sleek and fast ships that were a combination of the new and the old. Though the hulls were made of iron, the huge vessels, now called steamships, or "steamers," still carried full masts, rigging, and sails (which allowed the steamers to use good weather and wind, thereby decreasing fuel

RMS Atlantic *breaking up, 1873*

consumption). Several coal-fired boilers generated plenty of steam power to increase speed.

The White Star Line prided itself on the unrivalled first-class opulence of its ships. The dining rooms, lounges, saloon, and staterooms featured only the finest appointments in furnishings and adornments. The focus of each Atlantic crossing was speed, comfort, and luxury. So it was with the *Atlantic*, the pride of the White Star Line. Along with its sister ships, the *Baltic*, *Oceanic*, and *Republic*, the *Atlantic* was poised to dominate the transatlantic passenger trade for years to come. Unfortunately, no one could foretell the great disaster that was to befall the liner in 1873.

The *Atlantic*, built in Northern Ireland in 1871, was an iron-hulled, four-masted barque of 3,390 tons, designated as a mail carrier as well as a passenger ship. Powered by four compound cylinders using eleven boilers, the ship was able to put out six hundred horsepower on its single propeller. Built with six watertight bulkheads, the *Atlantic* was also equipped with auxiliary sail, and, with a ten-to-one length-to-beam ratio, the ship was designed for speed.

On March 20, the *Atlantic* sailed out of Liverpool, England, for its nineteenth time, bound for New York. On board were 952 people, including 700 steerage passengers, and almost 200 children. Eleven days later, on March 31, most of the way into an uneventful voyage, the coal engineer reported that the coal reserve was getting unusually low. Not wanting to take the risk of running out of coal should they hit a gale, Captain Williams decided to head for Halifax, about 170 miles distant. Making a few course corrections as they neared the Nova Scotia coast, and encountering storm conditions and high seas, the *Atlantic* drew closer to Halifax, running straight at twelve knots and in total darkness. Visibility was extremely poor. Incredibly, extra lookouts and depth sounders were never used in the *Atlantic*'s approach.

The ship paid a terrible price for these omissions, when, at about 3:00 AM, it struck Mar's Head, near Mosher Island and close to the tiny village of Prospect. Grounded fast, the ship keeled wildly to port as the seas crashed in over its decks, smashing and sweeping away all the lifeboats on the port side, and at the same time making the starboard lifeboats impossible to access. The ship was filling up fast, so all the steerage and remaining passengers were

Looking for bodies, 1873

brought on deck and sent up to the rigging lest they be swept from the deck in the pounding, relentless surf. The weather was frigid with below-freezing temperatures and gale-force winds. Hundreds died from exposure in the rigging. Rope lines were set up from the battered ship to the mainland, a distance of about fifty yards, and about two hundred passengers managed to get off to safety this way.

Many others failed in their efforts and drowned. A desperate attempt was made to contact villagers, and one fisherman and

Services at the mass burial, 1873

his family struggled heroically the rest of the night, saving many lives from the doomed *Atlantic*. By morning other larger ships had arrived, and 390 survivors were taken to warmth and safety. However, 562 passengers on board perished, either in the rigging or from drowning, including all but one of the women and children.

A government inquiry concluded that the blame for the disaster rested on the shoulders of Captain Williams, who disregarded proper sailing procedures, especially when sailing in unknown waters in a gale with poor visibility. Today, resting in twenty to ninety feet of water, the remains of the RMS *Atlantic* are a favourite spot for divers and relic seekers. Several artifacts of the wreck have been recovered and are on display at the Maritime Museum of the Atlantic in Halifax.

1873 METHANE GAS BLOWS UP THE DRUMMOND COLLIERY

On May 13, 1873, the miners at the Drummond Colliery in Westville, Nova Scotia, had just returned to work following a brief strike, when a gas explosion rocked the mine. It was the worst gas-related coal-mining disaster yet seen in North America.

Methane gas, volatile as it is, was standard material for the workers, who could handle it by burning it off carefully in small amounts. Often found in small pockets within the coal seam, the gas is released when the face is mined, then dispersed or burned off quickly. On occasion these pockets of gas are quite large and are not ventilated rapidly enough, taking fire instead. Sometimes these fires can be quite large and difficult to extinguish. The real danger in a mine like the Drummond Colliery lay in the main slopes and shaft. If gas was allowed to build up in these areas, a dangerous condition could develop into disaster and then into tragedy in a split second. In the case of the Drummond mine, it was later assumed that gas had accumulated as a result of a massive malfunction of the ventilation system.

On the morning of May 13, Robert McLeod went to work as usual. During the morning he fired two powder charges at the coal face to loosen the coal. Neither shot ignited the released gas. Near noon he fired another shot, which ignited the gas—not an unusual occurrence, except that after fifteen minutes of fighting the fire it was still burning. At this point the men had to retreat because of dense smoke. After getting some fresh air, the miners returned, only to find that the fire had spread to the brattice, heavy curtain-like cloths used to control and direct ventilation. There was too much smoke to use the water pumps. The mine manager,

The first great explosion, 1873

John Dunn, was called in, saw that the situation was critical, and quickly ordered the area cleared of men.

But it was too late. A few moments later, at about 12:15 PM, the main shaft exploded. Debris, equipment, and bodies spewed violently out of the head frame slopes and air pits. Wood, coal, and stone were thrown, like an enormous cannon shot, 650 feet into the air, falling and smashing through buildings and roofs. Rumblings and explosions continued all day. One especially wicked blast on the following day, which many witnesses likened to a volcanic eruption, caused the land to tremble for miles around. The terri-fied villagers, not knowing when the destruction would end, could only hope and pray that their loved ones might somehow have survived the terrible ordeal. Firefighters from the surrounding areas of Pictou and New Glasgow, as well as many people from

Westville Miners' Monument

nearby rural areas, all worked together in suppressing the fire. The shafts were eventually filled with earth and sealed.

Sixty miners were lost in the disaster, leaving forty-five grieving widows and scores of fatherless children. Even mine manager John Dunn, who had bravely descended into the mine to help others after the first explosion, perished in a subsequent blast. It was said that every family around the Westville area lost a relative or friend to the tragedy. A coroner's inquest a few days after the catastrophe concluded that the explosions were caused by the disruption of ventilation airflow brought on by the fire in Robert McLeod's work area. This resulted in a quick and extreme buildup of methane gas throughout the main slopes of the pit. Even though the Acadia Coal Mine, near Westville, was still in operation, the Drummond disaster was considered a traumatic setback for the economy, as the mine was extremely profitable and the Intercolonial Company, which owned the colliery, was considered to be in a "flourishing condition." After being flooded and shut down for a year, the mine reopened, eventually expanding its operations by adding coke ovens, a coal washer, and a brick plant. The Drummond Colliery was back in business, and remained so for many years, employing eight hundred workers at its peak.

As a memorial to the miners who perished at the Drummond mine in 1873, and to other workers who lost their lives in separate mining accidents, a beautiful sixteen-foot-high monument—the tallest and oldest in the province found outside a cemetery—was erected by employees of the Drummond Colliery in October of 1891 in Miners Park. The monument was built by William Mackenzie and the carving done by James King. Inscribed on the base of the elegant statue are the names of all the miners lost in the Drummond mine.

1877 SAINT JOHN GOES UP IN FLAMES

In 1877, Saint John, New Brunswick, was a thriving city of fifty thousand citizens, ranked as one of the top four shipbuilding

The Victoria Hotel in ruins, 1877

centres in the world. Its busy port facilities were second to none on a global scale. Because the business and trade industries were booming, many wealthy merchants and lumber and shipbuilding barons settled in Saint John in newly constructed, opulent houses. The city abounded with banks, hotels, churches, and government and public buildings.

On June 20 of that year, fire broke out in an unassuming way. A simple spark, coming from either a nearby shop or sawmill (it was never determined) fell into a pile of dry hay. But when the burning hay was finally discovered, the fire was on the verge of being uncontrollable, with a strong wind fanning the flames.

Sadly, city budget cutbacks may have aided the further spread of the fire. Ten years earlier, the City of Saint John had decided to modernize its fire department. The city hired paid crews, did away with volunteer brigades, and purchased five new state-of-the-art steam-driven pumpers. Costs began to mount when the fire department realized that to be in a constant state of readiness, the machines had to have a head of steam maintained at all times. This meant much more manpower and extra costs. Stables had to be built for the many horses used to haul the heavy wagons, and with the added maintenance of these animals, the department budget was becoming severely strained. The department finally decided to save money by sharing its horses with the road crews in the public works department. This short-sighted decision may well have cost the fire department a city.

In its early stages, the fire probably could have been beaten by two fire engines, but precious time was lost trying to find the horses and rig the engine. Although engine No. 3 was at the scene in three minutes, it took engine No. 2 almost an hour to arrive. By that time half a dozen buildings were already ablaze, and the fire was totally out of control. Several other engines arrived eventually, but there was little they could do. The city of Saint John was now at the mercy of the unforgiving wrath of flame and wind.

Nine and a half hours later it was all over but the shock and sorrow. For many looking out over the smoking ruins of the devastated city, only a weary sadness remained. At least nineteen people died as a result of the fast-moving fire, and scores were seriously injured. The property loss was valued at a staggering twenty-eight million dollars, only about a quarter of which was covered by insurance.

Looking west from Germain Street, 1877

Looking west from Queen's Square, 1877

Two hundred acres of prime residential and commercial land lay in ruins. Eight beautiful churches were destroyed, as well as fourteen hotels, six banks, and numerous public buildings. In all, more than sixteen hundred buildings were reduced to charred, smoking ash heaps.

Relief efforts began immediately. Most of the city's medical supplies and food had been lost when the warehouses were destroyed, so priority was put on medical aid, food, and shelter. The Victoria skating rink served as a shelter for a number of days, and temporary tents were erected. Relief societies were efficiently organized as money and aid supplies began pouring in from all over the globe. Within a year the city had well over thirteen hundred new buildings constructed, with many of the civic and public buildings made of stone or brick. Needless to say, extremely stringent fire regulations were enforced. Over the next decade, the prosperous merchants and businessmen tried to outdo each other in rebuilding their mansions in a grand period of rebirth and renewal.

1891 A MASSIVE MINE EXPLOSION ROCKS SPRINGHILL

In 1820, on a beautiful verdant Nova Scotia hillside abundant with cold, clear water from its many natural springs, a small group of Loyalists founded the small settlement of Springhill. Coal had been discovered in the area many years before, when Ludwig Hunter ran a small mine to sell coal to the local blacksmiths. In the early 1860s both Nathan Parks and William Simpson also ran small mining operations. Ten years later the Springhill Mining

The mangled bodies of pit ponies, 1891

Company was formed to supply coal for the Intercolonial Railway locomotives. It was the age of steam-driven machinery, and the great engines with their huge coal-fed boilers had an insatiable appetite. Coal became an extremely precious commodity, and as demand increased, more and more mines were developing into large-scale operations, especially in the extensive coal-rich counties of northeastern Nova Scotia. Springhill went big time in the 1880s with five mines producing over two thousand tons per day. Employment was created for more than thirteen hundred men and, unfortunately, children, as labour laws in place before 1923 permitted boys as young as eight years old to work in the pits. In a fifteen-year period from 1873 to 1888, the population swelled from two hundred to over five thousand as the town became more prosperous. In 1889 Springhill was incorporated as a town and was recognized as the hub of Cumberland County.

THE EXPLOSION

The tough miners who worked the Springhill collieries, among the deepest in the world, were well aware of the many hazards of underground coal mining. The risks were always there—a coal dust explosion could be ignited by the tiniest spark, as could the volatile methane gas. Just breathing the poisonous afterdamp gas could be fatal in seconds. And the miners were always aware of the reality of a mine-shattering "bump." A coal mine bump occurs when a buildup of rock pressure against the supporting tunnel pillars suddenly bursts through with explosive force, often causing the floor and ceiling of the tunnel to slam together, usually fatal to anyone working that area.

So, for the most part, the coal miners' lives depended on reliable gas detection, a secure ventilation system, and as much luck as their God was willing to dole out. A major incident had never yet occurred at the Springhill mine, although there had been a few individual fatalities. The Pictou and Cape Breton collieries had experienced tragic explosions in previous years, but the men of Nos. 1, 2, and 3 collieries in Springhill were making a good life for themselves. On February 21, 1891, that would change for 125 miners when catastrophe struck hard.

The men beginning the day shift were in good humour as they descended into the ink-black darkness, knowing that the mine had just been given an excellent grade in its safety inspection the previous day. A few employees were a bit nervous over a disaster prediction by a local seer, but even that wasn't supposed to happen until May. Still, it was not the kind of thought any coal miner wanted to carry down into the depths with him. Morning passed quickly, noon came, and most of the men who were working the 1,300-foot level paused for their half-hour break, some grabbing

An illustration of a rescue party in a mine, undated

their lunch pails for sandwiches and cups of tea. The men were unaware of the deadly coal dust buildup on No. 1 and No. 2 slopes. It was never determined exactly what sparked the fatal blast, but at approximately 12:30 PM the coal dust ignited and a massive explosion swept through both No. 1 and No. 2 collieries (shafts). The faint tremor felt on the surface belied the death, destruction, and terror going on deep below.

One hundred and twenty-five miners died, most of them killed outright. As described by survivors, the blast came in three stages. First, the explosion displaced the air, sending it rushing with tornado-like force down the tunnels, throwing, twisting, and tearing away anything in its path. Next came fireballs of all sizes, just before the main rush of all-consuming, vicious flames, which completely filled the tunnels, destroying almost everything left in its path.

Everything happened within split seconds and for most of those lost, death was sudden and swift. Rescuers related that many of the bodies they found had peaceful looks on their faces, some with food still in their mouths, as though they were in mid-chew. In one case, a pipe was still in the victims' mouth, locked in a death grip.

THE RESCUE

Rescue efforts began right away. Pitiful pleas for help filled the darkness as the rescuers made their way tentatively through tangled heaps of wreckage. Many of those who managed to survive were found furthest from the blast suffering from burns, broken bones, and shock, and were taken quickly to the surface. Progress was extremely slow because of the twisted masses of equipment and piles of collapsed rubble, along with the ever-present danger of afterdamp gas. The rescuers despaired of finding any other person alive, such was the extent of the damage. Many bodies were found crushed, buried, or horribly burnt. Workers of all ages died, including several as young as thirteen, and one lad only twelve years old. As families gathered to identify loved ones brought to the surface, hope soon turned to bitter despair as the number of dead mounted. In several cases families lost a father and several sons together. Fifty-seven widows were left to mourn, along with 169 children.

THE INQUIRY

An inquiry was held, but it could not determine what caused the fatal spark that triggered the coal dust explosion. Inspectors insisted that the mine was safe, having just completed an exhaustive underground inspection that found gas and coal dust levels to be normal. They also declared that the Springhill collieries had adopted the most modern safety precautions, including many not found in other coal mines. Though it didn't particularly ease the mourners' grief, the explosion was declared accidental, absolving the mine owners and management of any responsibility.

1892 SEALERS STRUCK BY A FREAK STORM AT TRINITY BAY

Newfoundland's coastline, with its numerous coves, bays, and bights, has extremely unpredictable weather, although experienced fishermen and seafolk are for the most part very adept at reading the signs of approaching storms. Nonetheless, when it comes to Newfoundland weather, nothing is guaranteed. The hardy fisherfolk of the Trinity Bay area can attest to the fickleness of fair weather after a tragic sealing disaster in 1892 on a day that seemed so calm at the start.

February 1892 was a great month for seal hunters in the Trinity Bay area. Nearing the end of the month, the weather had held pleasant and many seals were on the ice floes, and close enough to shore that land hunters could reach them in day hunts. These landsmen (as opposed to the ship sealers) were quite successful during the month, having taken many tons of fresh seal meat while the weather held. Saturday, February 27, dawned bright and sunny, a perfect day to be outdoors. Heavy clothing didn't seem necessary, as the blue sky and warm sun combined with calm seas that blew hardly any wind at all. One would have to be foolish or downright lazy not to take advantage of such fine weather, especially when the bay was full of loose ice and loaded with basking seals. A half-day on the floes would supply many with meat for months to come. So, many of the men from the outports took to their dories and small boats and headed for the seal heads. A great many of the men, anxious to get started, were dressed only in light clothes and brought no food along, planning to be back home within a few hours. The disastrous events that soon followed proved that weather in this area could not be taken for granted.

The boats out on the bay were from various ports along the coast: English Harbour, Port Rexton, Bannister, Green Bay, Deer Harbour, Champney, Ireland's Eye, and Trinity South. Some boats were fairly close to shore, while others were out quite a long distance. At around eleven o'clock the weather changed drastically. The wind picked up, blowing north-northeast, while the sea chopped into whitecaps and grew wilder. The temperature dropped quickly to below freezing. Fierce squalls lashed the small dories with freezing salt spray. The boats nearest land made for any shore they could find. Those farther out had to row head-on into the gale-force winds, the men without proper clothing growing numb with cold. Rowing desperately for up to five hours into the terrible northeast winds, the men gradually inched towards shore. When they finally reached land, some had already died in the boats. Others were totally exhausted and too numb to even speak.

Several of the men on land went to the Horse Chops area where they spotted some boats desperately trying to reach shore. John

A typical Newfoundland sealing village, c.1900

Butler, Robert Penny, Robert Ivany, and Stephen Day struggled selflessly for hours trying to get the wet and freezing men up over the sea cliffs to warmth and safety. Some of the boatmen were completely encased in ice. For several of the men in this group of boats, it was too late to be saved, despite the heroics of their determined rescuers. Other boatloads of men managed to get ashore at Trouty, Bonaventure, and Deer Harbour, where the residents were waiting to provide medical attention. Other residents, bravely facing the freezing winds, went out in their own boats to look for others still out in the bay. Communications being relatively primitive in those days, it was at least a full day before major centres heard about the disaster. Eventually, on the following Monday, and after another ship, the *Ingraham*, had retreated due to heavy ice, the government sent out the *Labrador* on a search mission. Although the *Labrador* was a more powerful steamer and carried a doctor on board, extreme ice conditions in Trinity Bay forced the rescue ship to retreat back to St. John's. Of course, in the aftermath there were charges that the government was too slow in starting a rescue mission. The general public was shocked and stunned by the immensity of the tragedy and relief funds poured in from all over Newfoundland and Canada. In all, of the two hundred men who hoped to enjoy a pleasant day on a minor seal-hunting excursion, twenty-four would pay the ultimate price in a deadly battle for survival against the unpredictable Newfoundland weather.

1892 FIRE DESTROYS ST. JOHN'S AGAIN

The worst disaster ever to befall the city of St. John's, Newfoundland, occurred on July 8, 1892, when a catastrophic inferno consumed most of the city, including the shopping districts and dock facilities. The death toll, fortunately, was limited to only three people, but the destruction of property and goods would amount to over twenty million dollars. A series of delays and somewhat comedic circumstances enabled the fire to get a good hold on the city and eventually overpower firefighting attempts.

June had been a hot and dry month, and the high temperatures carried over into July. The shingled roofs of the city's thousands of wooden dwellings were becoming dangerously dry under the blazing sun. On July 8 the temperature peaked at a much higher than normal eighty-five degrees Fahrenheit, and a strong arid wind was blowing across the city. The fire department had had a drill the day before and assumed they were well prepared for any breakout. Late in the afternoon, Thomas Fitzpatrick was in Timothy Brine's barn on Freshwater Road on a hilltop overlooking

St. John's in ruins following the Great Fire, 1892

A view of the ruined city looking towards the Narrows, 1892

downtown St. John's. Fitzpatrick was enjoying a good smoke when he inadvertently stumbled and dropped his pipe, the hot ash falling onto some loose, dry hay. Once again, careless smoking led to a raging inferno.

In a flash, a fire too large to stomp out grew quickly out of control, the barn a mass of flames. An alarm was sounded, but it took the volunteer fire brigade a long half-hour to respond. When the steam engine finally arrived, the firefighters discovered they had forgotten some important equipment, and even worse, a fire crew had neglected to fill the neighbourhood's water supply tank after a previous fire drill. During this time the fire was spreading, but most still believed it could be contained in the immediate neighbourhood. Things grew much more serious when it was discovered that there was not enough water pressure in the mains to supply the hoses because the city water had been shut off for most of the day so that new lines could be installed. Although they were turned back on later in the afternoon, the mains had not built enough pressure to supply the hilltop fire. Aided by a strong northeast wind, the fire was spreading by the second, sending sparks and flaming debris in all directions. The tragedy of errors continued when the firefighters discovered they could not tear down walls or roofs because they had forgotten to bring hatchets and axes with them.

To make matters even worse, the ropes the firefighters attempted to use were rotten and kept breaking. The horrified citizens tried desperately to save their personal belongings by packing valuable possessions into churches and public buildings, hoping the thick stone walls would stop the flames. It didn't work, as roofs collapsed into flaming heaps, completely destroying everything in the buildings. The fire was now raging and racing down Freshwater Road. Eventually, the fire split, one front heading west and the other wiping out everything in its fiery advance eastward. In its path lay the heart of the city, the business and commercial district, and the busy dockyards. With an extraordinary effort

Remains of homes near the waterfront, 1892

of desperation and sweat, the westward progress of the fire was eventually halted by tearing down a row of buildings, and only the eastern front remained.

Into the night, the inferno raged. Already lost were street after street of residential dwellings. Also fallen to the tempest were the Anglican Cathedral of St. John the Baptist, the Gower Street Methodist Church, the Masonic Temple, St. Andrew's Church, and the Court House and Athenaeum, which housed a beautiful library as well as several government agencies. Telegraph offices went down in flames, effectively cutting St. John's off from the outside world.

The firefighters and citizens were eventually completely overpowered by the great conflagration. All they could do now was try to keep themselves alive. One after another, stores, warehouses, and businesses all along Water Street were devoured by the blaze. Flames shot high into the air as flammable oils, tars, and paints

The St. John's waterfront after the great fire, 1892

ignited warehouse stock, winter supplies, coal heaps, and grocery stores. One store alone, belonging to George Knowling, lost over 160,000 dollars in stock. Several ships that had not moved out of harm's way caught fire and burned at their moorings

When morning finally arrived, the exhausted, shocked, and horrified citizenry looked out upon a smoking ruin. Eastern St. John's was simply gone, its landscape now desolate and dotted with skeletal chimneys and collapsed and smoking walls. Thirteen thousand people were left homeless and had nothing except the clothes they wore.

Government relief began immediately. Tents were set up and sheds constructed for those who had no relatives or friends to stay with. Committees were quickly formed as supplies and money began to pour in from across Canada and other countries, including

Great Britain and the United States. Almost half a million dollars was eventually received by the St. John's Relief Committee. Rebuilding began immediately, and free lumber was given to many of the homeless to construct new homes. Larger edifices and new churches and municipal buildings were raised using modern architectural designs; many of these are now registered heritage buildings and are cherished by residents and visitors of St. John's.

1898 SS *GREENLAND* TRAPPED IN THE ICE

THE SEALERS

Newfoundland sealers have always been known for their fun-loving, outgoing, sometimes boisterous, but mostly genial, nature. But behind this exterior shell is a resilient, courageous, and tenacious man of the sea, ready and willing to take on the might of the savage Atlantic so that he might provide for his family. Indeed, for generations the welfare of Newfoundlanders depended on the short but lucrative seal pelt harvest each spring as a supplement to the fishing industry.

Each March, on a set day, boats would leave St. John's by the dozen, amid calls of farewell and good luck from the families and citizens cheering and waving wildly on the wharf. Optimism was always high on these departure days and every captain and sealer on board was eager to be the first back home, hopefully with a record-breaking bumper harvest of seal pelts. Families left behind were well aware of the weather hazards the sealers faced, and unspoken was the underlying fear of many on shore that one or more

Leaving for the ice fields, c.1902

loved ones would not be returning. But on the sunny morning of March 10, 1898, all seemed well. About a score of sealing ships, each weighing about two hundred tons, set out for the ice floes of northeast Newfoundland. Among them was the SS *Greenland*.

Built in Scotland in 1872 for its Canadian owners, the *Greenland*, a 250-ton steamer out of Bonavista Bay North, enjoyed several record-breaking years in the seal harvest. Bumper trips were common for the *Greenland*, which enjoyed the advantage of having extremely able and experienced captains over its thirty-five-year career. At the start of the 1898 seal hunt, the ship was under the trusted command of Captain George Barbour, a well-known and well-liked skipper with years of experience. On March 12, a large herd, estimated at sixty thousand pelts, was sighted northeast of the Funk Islands. Four of the ships—the *Aurora*, the *Iceland*, the *Diana*, and the *Greenland*—spread out, picking their spots. At midnight, March 14, the season officially opened, and Captain Barbour immediately ordered his men onto the floes to begin panning (that is, harvesting the pelts on the ice, then stacking and flagging the piles that were to be picked up later). Each ship had its own identifying flag. The harvest went smoothly for the crew of the *Greenland*; they had panned over twenty thousand seals by mid-morning of March 21. Problems arose some time later when it was time to start collecting the panned seals. Ten thousand, or fully half of their flagged harvest, could not be found. The men assumed that either the ice had shifted drastically or, more likely, the pelts had been stolen by another ship's crew.

On March 21, Captain Barbour ordered all his men, 154 in number, back out onto the ice, hoping to make up for his losses. Four groups, or watches, were spread out over a seven-mile-wide area. The *Greenland* stayed in an open area, or "lake," in the ice.

THE STORM

The day had started off calm and clear, and many of the sealers wore lighter clothing. But by late afternoon the darkening sky and heavy clouds signalled an approaching storm, and two hours later the winds had risen to gale force, the temperature dropping to well below zero. By this time Captain Barbour was attempting to pick up his men. The first group got aboard safely, but in attempting to reach the remaining men, the *Greenland* was stopped by an impenetrable barrier of thick ice. A three-mile open channel also prevented the sealers from walking back to the ship. From that moment on, it became a desperate fight for survival, as the brave but hapless sealers struggled gamely to hang on until help arrived.

The bitter cold, aided by hurricane winds and blinding snow, proved fatal to many. The fast-weakening sealers were completely at the mercy of the elements. Those without oilskins or heavy garments perished quickly. Those who were stranded on "rough ice"

Newfoundland sealing captains, 1902

had it a bit easier: they could, at least, build a snow shelter. Others were able to build small but life-saving fires using bits of tarred rope and wooden gaff handles. One man found a seal, alive and warm, and used its body heat to stay alive. Another was able to stay alive by smearing seal blood thickly over his extremities. One sealer, giving up hope, lay down and pulled snow around him, hoping to create a final resting place. That act provided insulation and saved the young man's life. For many, the situation was hopeless. Stumbling around in the blinding snow, unable to see more than a foot ahead, several staggered into ice fissures and breathing holes. As the men grew colder, the final symptoms of hypothermia surfaced, and men became sleepy, weak minded, and feeble. Hallucinations were common. In one case, a sealer came running, urging the men to get up quickly and start signalling for the boat he had just seen. The languorous men, near their last, started yelling and jumping to attract the unseen boat's attention before finally realizing that the poor fellow must have been seeing things. Nonetheless, it got the men moving for a while, enough to save their lives.

THE RESCUE

Captain Barbour tried desperately to reach his men that night, but the strong gale blew the *Greenland* over leeward at such an angle that the cargo shifted, effectively trapping the ship in an almost horizontal position. The few men remaining on board laboured all night to reposition the cargo and supplies, until at last the *Greenland* was able to make headway. By mid-morning fifty men suffering from severe frostbite and hypothermia had been recovered. A head count was taken and the anguished captain acknowledged that there were still fifty-two men out on the ice. Of these, only four were found alive. Twenty-three bodies were recovered, and twenty-five sealers were never found and were assumed drowned. Abandoning the sealing trip, the *Greenland* turned for home, the bodies of the victims stacked like cordwood along the decks.

It was not to be an easy trip back. Forced by a storm to take shelter near Bay de Verde, the *Greenland* broke its moorings and drifted, only to ground itself on some deadly rocks. By shifting the freight around once again, the sealers were able to refloat the ship five hours later. Their bad luck continued, however, when they encountered dense fog and nearly ran aground on the Biscay rocks. Finally, on Sunday morning, March 27, the death ship slowly passed through the Narrows of St. John's Harbour, its flag flying at half-mast. Huge throngs of people, having heard of the disaster

Sealers panning and flagging seals, undated

by telegraph, crowded the docks and looked on in silent grief as the *Greenland* brought in its macabre cargo for unloading.

THE INQUIRY

As the citizenry came to know the full story behind the tragedy, the demand for a public inquiry grew. Questions had to be answered. Who was at fault here? Did Captain Barbour wait too long before picking up his men? Was this greed? Were the missing pelts stolen? Why wasn't Captain Barbour using proper signals to notify other ships of the tragedy? And why did Abram Kean, captain of one of the other sealing vessels, not help in the rescue?

The inquiry heard contradictory claims. Barbour said he put his men out two hours later than the other ships, so he stayed longer. Abe Kean, of course, denied stealing pelts, but others claimed they saw his men doing so. Kean also claimed he did not know that the ship's crew was in distress, as there was only one flag flying at half-mast and nothing else indicating that help was needed.

The notorious Captain Abram Kean aboard the SS Nascopic, *c.1930*

Other captains said the same—surely an error of omission on Captain Barbour's part.

For some reason, the results of the inquiry were never published and the whole affair faded quickly from the public eye. It was assumed that both Barbour and Kean could ill afford to have their reputations tarnished for fear of losing their lucrative positions as skippers. Finally, the Newfoundland government, not willing to pass legislation to improve the sealers' working conditions lest the boat owners' profits be lessened, was only too willing to have the inquiry dropped.

The SS *Greenland* tragedy reveals the true intensity of the Newfoundland sealing industry at the turn of the century. Avarice, dishonesty, and disregard for the perils of nature resulted in the heartbreaking loss of forty-eight men in a tragic disaster that might well have been avoided.

PART TWO
1900–1950

A T THE DAWN of the twentieth century, Atlantic Canada was enjoying a period of relative contentment as our towns and cities flourished. The first half of the century would see great advancements in technology, especially in our methods of transportation. The development and popularity of the automobile would be followed a short time later by the airplane, while massive passenger-carrying ocean liners plied transatlantic routes on a regular basis. A dozen years into the new century, there had been no major disasters in Atlantic Canada. Unfortunately, that would soon change as a series of tragic incidents over the next seven years rocked the region, claiming thousands of lives.

It all began with the great *Titanic* tragedy in 1912, followed in 1914 by the sinking of the Canadian Pacific liner, the *Empress of Ireland*. Also in 1914, the dangers inherent in the sealing industry became apparent when two major disasters occurred during one of Newfoundland's infamous gales. In 1917, in New Waterford, Nova Scotia, the Dominion Coal mine exploded, killing scores of miners. Many felt the incident was a direct result of ignoring safety for increased production for the Allied war machine. Later in December of that same year, the Halifax Explosion occurred, decimating the North End of Halifax, an event so cataclysmic that it is considered the greatest and most infamous of all Canadian disasters. A year later, the passenger ship SS *Florizel*, out of St. John's, broke up on treacherous rocks near Cape Race, losing ninety-six passengers and crew. Despite great strides in boatbuilding technology, we still could not face the raging Atlantic without trepidation. In 1926, and again in 1927, savage August gales off the coast of Nova Scotia took scores of lives, destroying several ships that had the misfortune of getting caught in the vicious storms. In 1929, a huge tidal wave, generated by an undersea earthquake, was responsible for the destruction of numerous outports in the Burin Peninsula region of Newfoundland. Though sealers were well aware of the harsh working conditions involved in their industry, it did not lessen their grief, when, in 1931, the SS *Viking* blew up at sea when its powder magazine exploded. In 1936, through the advent of national radio broadcasting, the intense drama of the Moose River gold mine cave-in was brought to the nation.

World War I and II both occurred during the first half of the twentieth century and Atlantic Canadians were not immune to the heartbreak caused by those events' senseless acts of destruction. In 1942, the ferry SS *Caribou* was sunk by an enemy submarine. That same year two American warships, the *Truxtun* and the *Pollux*, ran aground on the rugged rocks near Lawn and St. Lawrence on the Burin Peninsula. Despite a heavy loss of life, the heroic rescue attempts by local villagers saved almost two hundred sailors. Also in 1942, and related to wartime activities, was the fiery destruction of the Knights of Columbus servicemen's hostel in St. John's. Although not proven, most people believed at the time that the tragic fire was a despicable act of sabotage.

By mid-century a new form of transportation was emerging as airlines able to cross continents were becoming more and more common, thereby increasing greatly the potential of disaster from our skies. Indeed, in 1946, thirty-nine people perished as a DC-4 airliner ploughed into a hillside shortly after takeoff from Harmon field, near Stephenville, Newfoundland.

Despite beginning on a rather optimistic note, the first half of the twentieth century eventually realized its share of sudden loss, heartbreak, sorrow, and outrage. And while the majority of disasters in this fifty-year period were weather related, at least seven involved wartime activities.

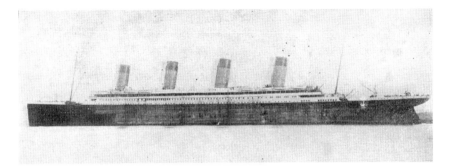

The great ship, 1912

1912 THE "UNSINKABLE" *TITANIC* GOES DOWN OFF NEWFOUNDLAND

THE SHIP

The sinking of the RMS *Titanic*, arguably the most famous sea disaster of them all, has long been the subject of books, films, dramas, and musical theatre productions. A variety of factors combined to make the sinking of the *Titanic* the superlative sea disaster. First of all, the *Titanic* was the finest boat afloat when it left its Southampton moorings for its maiden voyage to New York City. On board were many of the rich and famous of the golden age of ocean liners. John Jacob Astor, Isador Straus, and Benjamin Guggenheim were probably the best known among many of the wealthy first-class passengers who delighted in the splendour of the big ship. The pride of the White Star Line and jewel of its fleet, the 46,428-ton *Titanic* was, at that time, the largest ship in the world, almost nine hundred feet long and one hundred feet wide. Its seven decks carried all the facilities needed for a small city. The ship carried over 2,200 people, including crew and three classes of passengers.

With sixteen watertight compartments to keep the ship tight and safe, the *Titanic* was considered to be unsinkable. Because of this assumption, the ship carried only half the number of lifeboats necessary to serve all crew and passengers. Furthermore, lifeboat drills were deemed unnecessary. These would prove to be perhaps the most fatal of several errors and omissions that ultimately led to horrendous loss of life. William Smith, captain of the *Titanic*, was on his final run before retiring from the White Star Line. Wanting to prove the speed capabilities of the great ship, he undertook to make New York in record time. Warnings of an approaching iceberg field were given only a cursory thought as the liner sped recklessly along. There was no specific iceberg watch—another fatal error.

THE COLLISION AND SINKING

The evening of April 14 was calm and star-filled. Approaching midnight, many of the *Titanic*'s passengers had already retired for the night while others still strolled the decks enjoying the fresh evening air and watching in amazement as the huge ship slipped silently past enormous icebergs. As the great liner steamed towards its destiny, the band in the first-class section played on. Suddenly, a great shudder was felt ripping along the starboard hull of the ship. The *Titanic* came to a sudden stop. The ship had hit an iceberg and water was pouring into its forward compartments at an unstoppable rate. The ship's designer, Thomas Andrews, was quickly summoned. On inspecting the damage the iceberg had done to his ship, Andrews made the fatal pronouncement: the "unsinkable" *Titanic* had about two hours before it would be unable to stay afloat.

Most passengers were not aware that the great liner had hit an iceberg. Others just felt a brief shudder and gave it no second

A dory picking up bodies, 1912

thought. When the order to abandon ship and don lifejackets came, many refused, thinking it was just an emergency drill. Though there was no panic at first, the steadily tilting bow of the ship could not be denied. Following the policy of "women and children first," the lifeboats began to fill up, mostly with first-class passengers. Steerage passengers had to force their way on deck to reach the lifeboats. It soon became apparent that there would not be nearly enough lifeboats, and panic increased. Tearful farewells with husbands and loved ones ensued as more than a thousand passengers and crew, mainly men, realized that their fate was sealed unless rescue vessels arrived quickly. This was not to be, as the wireless operators tried in vain to contact other ships nearby. The *Carpathia* was reached, but that ship was too far away. The *California* was within sight of the *Titanic*, and had earlier tried to warn it of deadly icebergs in the area. When the warning went unheeded, the *California*'s wireless operator went off duty for the night. Flares the *California* later saw coming

Preparing bodies for burial, 1912

Awaiting victims at dockside, 1912

from the *Titanic* were assumed to be fireworks. When the great ship eventually disappeared, the *California*'s crew thought it had just steamed away.

At around 2:30 AM the *Titanic* was in complete chaos as it prepared to take its final plunge. As the sinking bow lifted the stern higher and higher, any movable objects slid and crashed down the decks. Many of the passengers still on board fell, slid, or jumped into the frigid North Atlantic waters. The screams of those left on deck mingled with those thrashing desperately in the icy water. It was pandemonium. Suddenly, the *Titanic*, its stern now nearly ninety degrees to the vertical, broke in two amidships, its bow going straight down to the depths. The stern, however, settled back down to an almost horizontal position, but only for a few moments until the water caught it. Again, the stern went straight up, then quickly down to follow the bow section of the ship. The *Titanic* was finally lost forever. For a while, cries and shouts of terror issued from those desperately trying to stay alive in the water, but these subsided as the deadly effects of hypothermia took over. Soon only silence remained.

Of the approximately 2,200 people on board the *Titanic*, 705 survived the sinking. The survivors were taken to New York by the *Carpathia*, while the dead were brought to Halifax. Several ships, including the *Minia*, the *Mackay-Bennett*, and the *Montmagny*, searched for bodies for several weeks after the disaster. Only 328 bodies were ever retrieved, and 1,200 people found their eternal resting place in the cold Atlantic Ocean. The loss of the *Titanic* showed once again that the arrogance of humans toward the forces of nature can be deadly.

1914 A BLIZZARD DEVASTATES THE SS *NEWFOUNDLAND*'S CREW

The greatest sealing tragedy in Newfoundland history occurred in 1914, when 115 sealers were stranded for fifty-three agonizing hours on the shifting pack ice, enduring a fierce blizzard and freezing temperatures. Seventy-eight men perished in this disaster, either by freezing to death or by drowning. Perhaps the saddest part of the tragedy is that it could have been avoided. It was a sad case of a catastrophic communications failure and poor human judgment involving the best-known sealing captain in Newfoundland: Captain Abram Kean.

In 1914 Captain Kean had already been involved in the sealing industry for almost fifty years, and his exploits were legendary. He began fishing at thirteen years of age and was master of his own ship at twenty-three. Kean commanded many vessels throughout the succeeding years in both the fishing and sealing industries, but his renown came from his sealing adventures. Kean held several seal harvest records, and eventually he became Newfoundland's first minister of fisheries.

The legendary captain was a hard-nosed, no-nonsense teetotaller who many believed would stop at nothing to bring home record harvests, even if it meant stealing panned and flagged pelts. Kean was involved in the *Greenland* sealing disaster of 1898; many questions regarding the captain remained unanswered from that incident, and the brash skipper became a pariah to many.

The 1914 tragedy involved two sealing ships: the *Stephano*, captained by Abram Kean, and the *Newfoundland*, skippered by none other than Kean's son, Westbury.

On March 30, the elder Kean, aboard the *Stephano*, signalled the *Newfoundland* that a large herd of seals was sighted. Not sure

The SS Newfoundland *and Captain Wes Kean (inset), c.1915*

where the seals were located, the younger Kean sent his men onto the ice, directing them to head for his father's ship, where they would be told the position of the seals. They were also informed that they were to spend the night aboard the *Stephano*.

Kean Sr. met the men, told them where the herd was to be found, but would not allow them to stay aboard his ship that night. Instead, he instructed them, despite indications of approaching severe weather, to head back to the *Newfoundland* once their day's work was done. Putting their trust into Kean, the sealers headed back out onto the ice. Before they could reach their own ship, they were caught in a severe blizzard. George Tuff, their second hand, or foreman, desperately tried to get his crew back to the

Sealers on the ice, undated

Newfoundland, but his men were not outfitted for the unexpected icy winds. There was no food, no fire, and hardly any shelter. Worst of all was the chilling thought that nobody back at the ships knew they were missing! Both the *Newfoundland* and the *Stephano* assumed the men were safely aboard the other ship, so there was no immediate concern and no rescue party. The doomed sealers began to succumb to their fate. Incredibly, thirty-seven men were able to survive the fifty-three-hour ordeal, but eleven of these men were permanently disabled, both physically and mentally. As in the 1898 *Greenland* disaster, the *Newfoundland* finally arrived back at its home port, bodies stacked on its deck, frozen and silent as statues in a museum. Hundreds were left to mourn and an immediate public inquiry was demanded.

So who was to blame for such a devastating and heartbreaking tragedy? A government inquiry eventually brought out a split ruling, partially blaming Abram Kean for his misjudgment, while also ruling the disaster an act of God. Kean returned to the seal hunt, not retiring until 1936. In his 1935 autobiography, the veteran sea captain maintained his innocence, insisting he followed proper protocol and placing blame on the lack of a wireless on the *Newfoundland*. Others who knew Kean say the terrible loss of life haunted him for the rest of his days. The *Newfoundland* sealing disaster of 1914 clearly showed, once again, that nature could not be trifled with, and that anyone who makes assumptions about the unpredictable and sometimes ferocious Atlantic weather risks tragedy, heartbreak, and loss.

1914 THE SS *SOUTHERN CROSS* DISAPPEARS WITHOUT A TRACE

The SS *Newfoundland* tragedy in March 1914, as heartbreaking as it was, turned out to be the lesser of two disasters occurring the same day and involving the same storm. The disappearance of the sealing ship SS *Southern Cross* and its crew of 173 marked the greatest number of men lost in a single Newfoundland sealing disaster—a sad end to a ship that had had a remarkable and adventurous career.

The *Southern Cross* was built in Norway in 1886 and for twelve years plied its trade as a whaler, going under the name of the *Pollux*. By 1898, and well into the age of the Arctic and Subarctic adventurers, the famous explorer Carstens Borchgrevink was in the market for a solid, reliable ship that could be refitted with engines and steam. In the *Pollux* the adventurer found his answer; over the next two years it proceeded to make history as the first boat to explore uncharted Antarctic territory, notably the Ross Sea.

SS Southern Cross, *c.1914*

In 1901 its exploration mandate now over, the *Pollux* was sold first to a firm in Scotland and then, in the same year, to the Baine and Johnson Company, which refitted the ship and brought it to Newfoundland to work the annual seal harvest.

Rechristened the *Southern Cross*, the ship proved its worth over and over again during the next fourteen years. Under the guidance of such stalwart and experienced captains as Darius Blandford and George Clarke, the *Southern Cross* brought home bumper harvests of seal pelts, ever determined to win the prestigious "silk flag."

The seal hunt went well for Captain Clarke and his crew in the spring of 1914. Leaving St. John's on March 12, the ship quickly found a herd of prime harp seals, and by March 29 over fifteen thousand pelts had been loaded on board. The somewhat ambitious Captain Clarke was determined to break the *Southern Cross*'s bumper crop record of sixteen thousand pelts, set the previous year, and so ordered more to be stacked on deck. The final tally was an estimated seventeen thousand seals. The young, relatively inexperienced crew headed home, the boat dangerously overloaded. The ship was even lower in the water as a result of the extra weight caused by the vessel's midship engine position. Communication with other ships would be difficult, as the aging vessel was not yet equipped with wireless, but instead used a system of whistles and flags to send messages. By March 29, the *Southern Cross* was sighted, heavily laden and running at full steam past Channel–Port aux Basques. About sixteen hours later the ship was seen by the *Portia* at the southern end of the Avalon Peninsula. It was battling a terrible storm, but answered the *Portia*'s whistle, indicating that everything was fine, and continued under a heavy head of steam, the bow dangerously low.

That was the last anyone saw or heard of the *Southern Cross*. After it failed to arrive at its home port, an intensive search was started in hopes of at least finding debris or some indication of what happened. Several vessels took part in the search, including the *Kyle*, the *Seneca*, and the *Fiona*. But nothing showed up positively identifying the ship and, after twenty days, the *Southern Cross* was officially declared lost along with the 173 men on board. A Sealing Commission inquiry officially called the disaster an act of God, while acknowledging that the inexperience of the crew, the excessive number of pelts on deck (which may have blocked the water holes), and a low-mounted engine may have contributed to the tragedy.

1914 THE *EMPRESS OF IRELAND* COLLIDES WITH THE *STORSTAD*

THE SHIP

The early decades of the last century can be considered the golden age of the ocean-going passenger liners. Before the advent of mass air travel, no expense was spared on the lavish arrangements of first-class travel, be it by rail or sea. The Cunard and White Star lines included such famous ships as the *Mauritania*, the *Olympic*, the *Lusitania*, and of course the most famous of all, the *Titanic*. Synonymous with grandeur, lavishness, and sleek design, these huge liners were the Rolls Royces of the sea.

On a slightly smaller scale were the ships of the global Canadian Pacific Railway Company. If Cunard and White Star had the Rolls, then CPR had a Cadillac with their Empress Liners, the foremost being the speedy *Empress of Britain* and the quietly efficient *Empress of Ireland*. CPR's steamships were on the Liverpool–Quebec City route, which linked the company's transcontinental railroad and hotel system that stretched across Canada to Vancouver then across the Pacific to Asia.

Although only three quarters the size of the *Titanic* at 570 feet and 14,191 tons, and with only two stacks, the *Empress of Ireland*, designed and designated as a mail carrier, was truly built for speed: the ship was capable of hitting twenty knots at full ahead. Learning from the *Titanic*'s errors, the *Empress* carried 2,200 life jackets and over 40 lifeboats for its 1,550 passengers. It also had twenty-four watertight doors closing eleven bulkhead compartments. Also built for comfort, the *Empress of Ireland* was truly a class liner, boasting a 3,800-square-foot dining room complete with a five-piece orchestra to entertain diners, a two-storey atrium,

The Empress of Ireland, *pride of the Canadian Pacific Line, 1914*

a six-hundred-volume library, and a first-class music room with an elegant Steinway grand piano. Although often compared to the *Lusitania* in its splendour, the *Empress of Ireland* chose to keep a low profile, letting its sister ship, the *Empress of Britain*, bathe in the glory of its own speed records. Since its launch in 1906, the *Empress of Ireland* had made ninety-five Atlantic crossings and could boast a perfect safety record, going about its duties with quiet efficiency. So it is with a great degree of irony that the *Empress of Ireland* would be forever associated with tragedy.

THE COLLISION

On a bright and sunny Friday afternoon on May 28, 1914, the excited passengers of the *Empress of Ireland* bid adieu to Quebec City as the great liner, under the able command of the highly respected and experienced Henry Kendall, slipped out of its moorings and headed down the St. Lawrence River. On board were 1,477 people, including crew. Among the first-class passengers were several notables, including the popular British actor Laurence Irving and his wife Mabel Hackney, the Canadian socialite Mrs. Ethel Paton, and the adventurer and big game hunter Sir Henry Seton-Karr. Also on the ship were 167 members of the Salvation Army who were headed for London to attend a worldwide Salvation Army congress. Most of the 138 children on the doomed liner were in the third-class lower decks, among the diverse cultural mixture of the working class.

As the sleek liner made its way down the mighty St. Lawrence, guided by its pilot, the late afternoon dusk gradually gave way to nightfall. The din and excitement of leaving port had diminished as passengers enjoyed a starlit after-dinner stroll along the wide decks. By 1:00 AM most passengers—and many of the crew—had retired to their cabins and were fast asleep, some with their cabin portholes left open to catch the fresh night air—this despite ship regulations that stated all portholes had to be closed when at sea. Captain Kendall was at the helm when, at 1:30 AM, he dropped his pilot off near Pointe-au-Père, just east of the town of Rimouski. At this point, two hundred miles up from Quebec City, the river widened considerably and navigation was much easier. The *Empress* was now on its own, keeping the starboard shore close. The ship encountered small patches of fog, none so thick as to cause undue concern.

At 1:38 AM Kendall spotted another ship off his starboard bow at about six miles distance. The captain made a few course corrections to ensure his ship would have plenty of time to head out to sea. This would mean passing the as-yet-unknown ship on its starboard side. A few minutes later an extremely dense fog bank rolled in, completely blotting out visibility and creating a feeling of uncertainty and confusion. Following nautical procedures pertaining to fog and reduced visibility, Captain Kendall went immediately astern, which meant reversing engines, thus slowing and stopping the ship. His intentions were immediately signalled to the oncoming ship by three long whistles and two more blasts when the ship was stopped. The approaching vessel answered back each time with one short blast acknowledging the captain's message. All seemed routine, but in such heavy mist, it was quite easy to feel nervous.

A few minutes later, the fog lifted a bit, and Captain Kendall looked up in absolute horror as a large ship loomed up on his starboard side, bearing directly down on the *Empress*. Too late to avoid a collision, Kendall ordered full ahead to starboard, hoping to sustain only a glancing blow and minimize damage. It was in vain. The approaching vessel was the *Storstad*, a Norwegian collier, low in the water with a full load, and built with icebreaking capabilities. The *Storstad*'s deadly reinforced bow sliced into the *Empress* amidships between its two stacks as easily as a knife through butter. The fatal wound to the *Empress of Ireland* was a hole, fifteen feet in diameter, penetrating twenty-five feet deep into the ship's engine room.

Water immediately poured in at sixty thousand gallons per second. In a few minutes the engine room was flooded, the crew fighting for survival. With the crew unable to close the watertight doors, the fate of the great liner was sealed. In desperation, Captain Kendall signalled the *Storstad* to stay in the wound if it could, thus affecting a plugging and delaying action until they could at least get near the shore and shallow water. But it was too late, as the *Storstad*, heavily damaged but still afloat, was already free of the *Empress*. Within four minutes, the loss of the engine room dynamos put the ship in darkness. It had begun listing heavily to starboard immediately after the collision, and ten minutes later the ship was lying on its side like a beached relic.

There was time for only one desperate, hurried SOS before power failed completely. The situation was hopeless for most of the passengers and crew in the lower decks. Many perished in their bunks as the mortally wounded ship keeled over. Some passengers, mostly first-class, scrambled out onto the listing hull, praying that it would stay afloat until help arrived. It was not to be. Four minutes later, the hapless passengers and crewmembers were thrown into the sea when the massive hull slipped beneath the waves, coming to rest in 180 feet of frigid water. Only nine lifeboats could be launched. Fortunately, the *Storstad* was able to pluck most survivors from the icy waters before they succumbed to the cold. Captain Kendall, thrown from the ship when it keeled over, was among the 465 who survived the ordeal. Lost were 1,014 souls, including 840 passengers, eight more than in the sinking of the *Titanic*. Of the 138 children on board, only 4 survived.

THE INQUIRY

In June 1914 an inquiry was convened at Quebec City. Accusations, charges, and counter-charges were angrily exchanged as both sides attempted to absolve themselves of all blame for the disaster. The chairman of the inquiry was Lord Mersey, who had presided over the *Titanic* inquiry. At the heart of the inquiry was the question of running lights and rights-of-way. The many lights on the liner may have confused the Norwegian crews, who claimed the *Empress* was showing a red light, denoting that its port side was visible.

Captain Kendall claimed vehemently that he stuck to his proper starboard course at all times. One crewmember testified that there was a steering problem with the *Empress*, causing it to wobble and turn erratically at times. Captain Andersen of the *Storstad* was adamant, insisting that the liner turned into his ship, thus causing the collision.

The Norwegian ship was ultimately found responsible for the disaster by the Quebec City inquiry, although an independent Norwegian inquiry absolved the *Storstad* of all blame. Neither side would compromise their position. It is doubtful whether anyone will ever know who was to blame. What is known for certain is that the heavy fog was the ultimate cause of the disaster.

AFTERMATH

In the scope of human history, a major disaster can be forgotten. In the case of the *Empress of Ireland*, the advent of a war that would eventually consume much of the civilized world quickly overshadowed Canada's greatest marine tragedy. An assassin's bullet in Sarajevo, the sinking of the great liner *Lusitania* by enemy torpedo, and the slaughter on the battlefields in Europe soon relegated the *Empress of Ireland* disaster to the obscure pages of forgotten history.

The cold hull lies deep underwater, most of its passengers still with it. Over the years, time, rust, and strong currents have taken their toll. Silt and sand have filled in most of the starboard rooms, and divers have pillaged most of the interior artifacts. As well, too many human remains have been taken by thoughtless treasure seekers. In 1998 the site of the *Empress of Ireland* tragedy was declared Canada's first underwater heritage site by the government of Quebec and has since benefited from government protection legislation.

1917 A WARTIME MINING ACCIDENT IN NEW WATERFORD

Like so many coal towns, New Waterford, Nova Scotia, has known the devastation of mine explosions. Indeed, the explosion at the Dominion No. 12 colliery on July 25, 1917, proved to be the most disastrous to date in the history of Cape Breton coal mining.

Canada and Europe were still in the grip of World War I, and demand for coal was heavy. Mine owners, trying to cash in on this bonanza, pushed their company officials to extract more coal, and to do it faster. Important and necessary safety precautions sometimes fell by the wayside as production targets became top priority.

The most vital safety factor in a coal mine operation is the ventilation and control of the methane found in every colliery. Gas in small pockets or amounts may not be fatal, but left unattended, it can build up to lethal concentrations. Good ventilation systems included fresh air being blown down the slopes continually, which helped clean contaminated air. Brattices, huge curtain-like canvas sheets, were also supposed to be used to help divert the methane (and fresh air) to the proper tunnels. In those days, brattices were absolutely necessary to run a safe and clean mine. The Dominion No. 12 colliery was already known as a gassy mine. From time to time, miners had to take a day or more off, complaining of feeling sick from the high gas levels. Some mornings the men would encounter hundreds of feet of methane buildup and could not work until the fans cleared the danger. In 1917 the company was on dangerous ground with its unspoken policy of production at any cost. The condition of the mine did not seem to worry the bosses as long as the coal got out. In short, the Dominion colliery was a disaster just waiting to happen.

A miner dressed for his underground shift

THE BLAST

At 7:30 AM on July 25, the day crew was just beginning its shift. Two hundred and seventy miners were toiling underground that fateful day, many of them working the No. 6 and No. 7 landings at about 2,100 feet underground. Suddenly, a huge and horrendous explosion ripped through the No. 7 landing, maiming, destroying, and killing everything in sight. Rescue workers later found the mangled bodies of many victims with heads and limbs torn away and charred to blackness by fire. Rescuers waited until midnight to bring up the remains of the worst cases, so as not to upset those hoping that a loved one might still be alive.

As if the explosion was not deadly enough, any survivors of the direct blast were now subject to the lethal by-product of methane combustion. Deadly concentrations of carbon monoxide gas filled the levels close to the blast area. Silent, odourless, and colourless, this killer gas accounted for many of the sixty-two fatalities.

Halifax newspaper headlines, July 26, 1917

Death from carbon monoxide poisoning is the opposite of a sudden explosion: it kills silently as its victim just nods off to an eternal sleep. Two young miners who took part in rescue efforts, Phillip Nicholson and John Cook, died from carbon monoxide poisoning, but not before managing heroically to save several other men from

Members of the New Waterford community gather at the mine site awaiting news, 1917

death. Carl Pietchieck, another brave young man, only seventeen years of age, died while attempting to rescue several fellow miners.

THE CORONER'S INQUEST

A coroner's jury was quickly empanelled and an inquest into the deaths of the sixty-five miners began. In its verdict, the panel found the men were indeed victims of a methane gas explosion, but could not pinpoint exactly what triggered the blast. Some blame was put on one of the victims, John D. MacKay, a shot-fixer, who, some testified, fired the shot that set off the gas. Many others disputed this. The inquest also found the mine officials to be grossly negligent in having allowed the methane to build up to lethal retention levels by ignoring established ventilation and brattice procedures.

A provincial inquiry was also held, with the mine owners denying all responsibility for the disaster. The presiding judge, a new Supreme Court appointee, was a former solicitor for the Dominion Coal Company and had once prosecuted the union's leader for libel. It cannot be proved that the judge was biased in this inquiry, but he quickly absolved the company and its officers of all blame, surprising very few.

1917 HALIFAX HARBOUR EXPLODES

THE CITY

In December 1917, Halifax was the busiest city in Canada. The Great War had been dragging on for four years and it would be almost another full year before peace was finally achieved. Meanwhile, the city of Halifax and its port were a beehive of activity, most of it related to the war effort. Convoys of troops, weapons, explosives, and related war matériel were either amassing and awaiting convoy in the sheltered Bedford Basin, or were just arriving from overseas. Warships, bristling with weapons, were a common sight in Halifax Harbour as they awaited convoy duty. The city also contained thousands of troops, many awaiting embarkation, some stationed in the Halifax Garrison. Civilians, many of whom came to Halifax to take advantage of the excellent employment opportunities, swelled the city's population from approximately 47,000 in 1912 to 60,000.

Ship movement in and out of the harbour was a daily affair, and most civilians barely gave ships a second glance unless there was an extraordinary event such as a collision or fire. In fact, with so

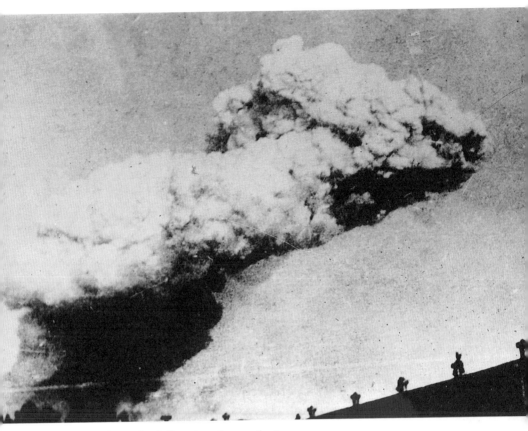

The cloud of smoke following the explosion, 1917

much traffic, collisions were quite common. A fire, though, was rare and more worthy of attention.

On December 6, on a beautiful sunny morning, the Norwegian vessel *Imo* had quietly slipped its moorings and was making its way toward the Narrows. The *Imo*, 430 feet long, was on its way to New York to pick up a load of relief supplies destined for Belgium. At around 7:30 that same morning, the three-hundred-foot *Mont Blanc*, a fully laden munitions ship, was proceeding to Bedford Basin to join up with a convoy heading overseas. Because of the danger of lurking U-boats, the ship was not flying any flag warning of its deadly cargo: almost three thousand tons of high-explosive chemicals and ammunition, including twenty-three hundred tons of picric acid, two hundred tons of TNT, thirty-five tons of benzol, and ten tons of guncotton.

THE EXPLOSION

At about 8:45 AM, the *Imo*, impatient and running behind schedule, struck the *Mont Blanc* on its starboard side. The collision was not severe, but it was enough to start a fire above deck on the *Mont Blanc*. The crew of the munitions ship immediately jumped in a lifeboat and started rowing madly for the Dartmouth shore, expecting their ship to blow up at any minute. The burning *Mont Blanc* drifted helplessly towards the Halifax shore in the industrial North End and began attracting attention. Crowds gathered along the docks to watch the thrilling spectacle of the flaming ship drifting towards the Richmond docks. Children on their way to school, shopkeepers on the waterfront, and workers and citizens of all ages and walks of life gazed intently, completely unaware of the tremendous disaster that was about to unfold.

Just before 9:05 AM, the *Mont Blanc* exploded with the force of a small nuclear blast. Historians estimate that the explosion was equal to one-seventh of the Hiroshima nuclear explosion that killed more than a hundred thousand people in 1945. The blast was felt as far away as Sydney, more than 270 miles away. Almost 1,600 people died quickly and the total number of dead would be over 1,900. Many of the victims' bodies were never found. The blast demolished every building near the waterfront, and any person who had gathered to witness the spectacular "fire" was killed instantly. Glass was shattered in every window in a fifty-mile radius.

Devastation on the Halifax waterfront, 1917

In fact, glass was responsible for as many as six hundred eye injuries. Thirty-seven people lost their sight completely, while 250 had to have at least one eye removed. Of the fifty thousand residents of the vibrant and teeming city of Halifax, twenty-five thousand were left homeless.

Property loss was over thirty-five million dollars. The *Mont Blanc* crew who so hastily departed their burning ship all survived, except one who died later in hospital from his wounds. The ill-fated munitions ship was so decimated by the blast that hardly any trace of it was found intact. Parts of it, including anchor and cannon, were found up to four miles away. Five crewmembers of the *Imo* also died that day, along with the ship's captain and pilot. To make matters worse, a severe snowstorm fell on the city the day following the explosion, hampering rescue efforts and further punishing those seeking shelter.

Looking towards Pier 8, 1917

THE AFTERMATH

Volunteers and relief money began pouring into the city almost immediately. Food, shelter for the homeless, and aid to the injured were organized by the quickly formed Halifax Relief Commission. Boston sent two trainloads of much needed medical supplies, as well as medical personnel. Doctors poured into Halifax by the hundreds from places as far away as Europe, Australia, and New Zealand. The survivors of the great blast opened up their homes to the homeless and destitute. Eventually the relief would reach a value of thirty million dollars, greatly helping the stricken city get back on its feet.

Understandably, the people of Halifax wanted answers. What happened and who was to blame for this massive explosion, the greatest the world had ever seen up to that time? A public inquiry was soon convened and the finger pointing started in earnest. The *Mont Blanc* was initially found to be responsible for the blast, but appeals soon prevailed. In the end, official blame was placed on both the *Imo* and the *Mont Blanc*. Though several individuals were initially charged with negligent manslaughter, these charges were later dismissed and no one was ever punished for any misconduct.

Today, memorial services are held annually throughout Halifax in commemoration of what must be considered the greatest disaster in Canadian history.

1918 SS *FLORIZEL* RUNS AGROUND AT HORN HEAD

Newfoundland has always depended on the sea, especially in times past. The sea and its bounty created employment for thousands of Newfoundlanders, and fishing was the only way of life for many. Fishing also provided much of the food for the people of Newfoundland. Moreover, for most of the tiny outposts scattered around the island, the sea provided the only means of transportation. Isolated as they were from the mainland, Newfoundlanders relied on the government ferries to go to and from the mainland. Larger sea-going ships sailed to larger centres such as Montreal, New York, and Boston. Though the sea was a part of Newfoundland life, this did not mean the sea was accommodating. At times the Atlantic could be terribly cold, cruel, and unforgiving,

SS Florizel *beginning its run*

often venting its fury on hapless vessels. It was difficult enough just to coexist with the volatile East Coast weather; to take it lightly could spell disaster. Numerous wrecks scattered along one of the most dangerous coastlines in the world can easily attest to the results of complacency.

The SS *Florizel* was one of the top passenger ships in the prestigious Red Cross Line and was owned by the huge Bowring Brothers organization from St. John's. Built in Scotland in 1908, the *Florizel* had icebreaking capabilities and was outfitted with the latest in wireless equipment. Plying its trade as a cargo vessel, but also used frequently in transportation service, the ship, valued at seven hundred thousand dollars, was skippered in 1918 by Captain William Martin.

On February 22, 1918, the *Florizel* was scheduled to sail from St. John's to New York via Halifax, but a huge winter storm had blown in that same day, delaying departure. From the safe moorings in the protection of St. John's Harbour, the weather did not look so bad, but just outside of port a nasty gale was blowing hard and visibility was extremely poor, making navigation difficult. Captain Martin knew this and normally would have delayed his sailing until the weather was somewhat better. But the issue was settled by one of the passengers, John Shannon Munn, a Bowring Company director. He selfishly insisted that the boat sail immediately, as he had an important meeting to attend in New York. Though the ultimate decision to sail belonged to the captain, intimidation was probably the overriding influence when Captain Martin sounded the farewell whistle and slowly began moving through the Narrows of St. John's Harbour into a maelstrom of wind, snow, and freezing ice.

The ship's crew of sixty was none too happy to be sailing in such stormy conditions. The *Florizel* also carried seventy-eight passengers, including several prominent businessmen and personalities from St. John's. The sailing was rough right from the beginning. Conditions were deteriorating so badly that Captain Martin, though an experienced seafarer, could not be absolutely sure of his position, nor could he be sure of his speed—a deadly combination that would have tragic consequences. Captain Martin assumed that he had already rounded Cape Race, on the southeastern tip of the Avalon Peninsula in Newfoundland, and adjusted his course to the southwest. Normally this would have put him on a direct course to Halifax.

But in fact, the *Florizel* had not yet reached Cape Race, and by turning to the southwest, the captain had put the doomed ship on a course towards the deadly rocks off Horn Head, Cappahayden. At around 4:40 AM on February 24, the *Florizel* hit the rocks at

SS Florizel *on the rocks at Cappahayden, 1918*

full speed, ripping its bottom badly, and grounding fast. The below decks filled fast and the raging surf washed over the listing deck in huge slashing waves as the frantic and terrified passengers ran in all directions seeking shelter from the raging storm. It would have been sheer folly to put lifeboats out in such a breaking sea.

Many passengers were swept off the decks to their death. Others jumped overboard and in desperation attempted to swim to shore, only to find the crashing surf too powerful. An SOS described the *Florizel* as helpless and "breaking up quickly." Several rescue vessels were immediately dispatched carrying plenty of blankets, medical supplies, and doctors. But the storm lasted almost another twenty-four hours, and no ship could get near enough to attempt rescue. Not until around 6:00 AM on February 25 was a rescue attempt made. By 8:00 AM, forty-four people had been rescued and were on their way to St. John's. The final death toll would be ninety-four passengers and crew.

The official investigation that soon followed the disaster heard testimony from fifty-four witnesses. Captain Martin was ultimately found to be responsible for the tragedy and was eventually suspended from his captain's duties for twenty-one months. If the captain had not bent to pressure from those who were responsible for his livelihood, it is very unlikely that this devastating tragedy would have occurred.

1926-1927 SAVAGE AUGUST GALES STRIKE TWO YEARS IN A ROW

AUGUST 1926

Life in the Atlantic Canadian fishery was never easy. Bountiful as the harvests may have been, each fishing excursion to the banks was fraught with danger, especially during the late summer and fall storm season. Sudden squalls had to be reckoned with, wind shifts threatened to push boats off course, and the freezing, salt-laced sea spray made life on deck miserable at times. And this was during relatively fair weather. Killer storms could form with only a few hours' notice, and hurricanes were always potential threats.

On August 7, 1926, a wicked late summer tropical storm caught two Nova Scotia fishing boats in its deadly grip. Several days after the storm, the schooner *Sylvia Mosher*, out of Lunenburg, was found washed up against the shores of Sable Island, its crew of twenty-six all missing. Further searching proved fruitless and the crew was deemed lost. Captained by John D. Mosher, the two-year-old boat was named after his young daughter. Meanwhile, the handliner *Sadie A. Knickle* also went missing after the

The Margaret K. Smith *racing for home, c.1922*

August 7 storm. Three weeks of scouring the Sable Island area revealed no trace of the ship or its crew of twenty-three, and eventually the search was abandoned. The tiny island had shown once again why it was known as the "graveyard of the Atlantic."

AUGUST 1927

On August 24, 1927, scores of fishing boats were hit by a sudden storm that struck the fishing waters of eastern Nova Scotia and Newfoundland without warning. Strangely, the sun was still brightly shining even though the wind was blowing at ninety miles

John D. Mosher, captain of the
ill-fated Sylvia Mosher, *c.1925*

per hour. Off the coast of Newfoundland, at least seven fishing schooners were lost, either by foundering and breaking up at sea or by being driven violently ashore.

In one case a captain had to beach his ship to save his passengers. Frantic searches were carried out as more and more boats were reported missing. Reports were slow to come in because communication had broken down between the village outports, and no one was sure exactly who or what ship was missing. Of the Newfoundland fleet, seven schooners were known to have gone down with all hands: the *Vienna, Hilda Gertrude, Annie Healey, Effie May,* and the *John C. Louglin.* As well, no trace of the *Loretta* or *Valena* ever showed up, and these two ships were also eventually deemed lost with all of their crews. Over forty lives were lost in this area of the storm alone.

Off Sable Island, the Lunenburg fishing fleet, which had recovered from the tragedy of the previous August, was decimated once again, this time with an even more horrendous loss of life. The *Mahala*, lost in the August 24 storm, carried a crew of twenty, many of whom were related to each other from the town of Blue Rocks. The fifteen crewmembers of the *Joyce Smith* were mostly from Newfoundland, but its captain, Edward Maxner, who had his two sons on board with him, was from Lunenburg. All were lost. The *Clayton Walters*, which was also eventually given up as lost, also had sons and brothers among the crew, mostly from Vogler's Cove. The *Ida Corkum* was the last of the schooners to be declared lost. The loss of the four Lunenburg boats was estimated to be worth nearly one hundred thousand dollars, a huge sum in those days. Even worse was the substantial loss of family income and its devastating effect on many of the surviving families. The Atlantic had claimed the 130 men, and in the process devastated the small communities they were from.

1929 A TSUNAMI SMASHES THE BURIN PENINSULA

The most populated areas of Newfoundland in 1929 were the Avalon and Burin regions. Relying on the fishing industry as a way of life, most residents lived in small picturesque villages with colourful names, like Ship's Cove, Rock Harbour, and High Beach. Though relatively infrequent in the region, earthquakes of major strength did (and still do) hit Atlantic Canada from time to time. A 7.2-magnitude earthquake in 1929 centred under the Atlantic Ocean triggered a severe tidal wave that caused great damage and loss of life in the Burin Peninsula area of Newfoundland.

The initial tremor was felt at 5:00 PM throughout the Atlantic provinces. Homes and buildings shook, glass rattled, and objects fell off shelves, but no real damage was reported. Initially, many thought their basement water boilers were malfunctioning and rushed down to look. The most serious damage was reported to be to the underwater telegraph cables, several of which were cut, leaving parts of Newfoundland, including the Burin Peninsula, without communication and effectively cutting them off from the rest of the island and mainland.

A monstrous tidal wave was generated by the undersea quake, and it got stronger and stronger as it rushed toward the unprotected west side of Placentia Bay at seventy-eight miles per hour. Reaching the narrowing at the bay's entrance, the wave crested at a fifteen-foot height and, two hours after the initial quake had occurred, slammed against the lower peninsula and viciously began working its way along the village-strewn coast.

The homes and buildings along this flat stretch of rugged shoreline were set close to the water. Though often pounded by surf and severe storms over the years, the buildings along the coast had never suffered any severe damage. This was about to change. The villages of Lawn, St. Lawrence, Great Burin, Fortune, Stepaside, and Collins Cove suffered terrible destruction to their waterfronts. Boats were ripped off their moorings, pushed inland, and smashed. Buildings located on docks and wharves were shattered into splinters before being washed out to sea. Warehouses, fishing gear, dories, coal supplies, and fish stocks were all destroyed or swept away.

A boat towing a house back to shore following the tidal wave, 1929

Rock Harbour lost everything, as did Ship Cove, Corbin, and
Lance au L'eau. Just about every village, hamlet, and settlement in
the tsunami's path was heavily damaged. While some villages were
situated in a position to deflect the wave, others took the assault
head on, with many deaths occurring as a result. At Point au Bras,
eleven homes were swept away and several people lost their lives,
including Henry Dibbon and his sister Mrs. Sam Bennett, Mrs.
Thomas Fudge and her three children, and Mrs. William Allan.

Point au Gaul fared no better. Almost seventy smaller buildings
were lost, along with several dwellings and all waterfront fishing
supplies. Heartbreaking was the loss of eight people, including
Thomas Hillier, Mrs. Henry Hillier and her four grandchildren,
and Mary Ann and Elizabeth Walsh. Taylor's Bay and Lord's Cove
were shattered, with fifteen families left homeless and destitute.

A house flattened by the tidal wave, 1929

As well, many people perished as they were swept away by the tsunami. Those lost included Bartholemew Bonnell and Mrs. Robert Bonnell and her two children. At Lord's Cove, Mrs. P. Rennie and three children were lost. At Kelly's Cove, Mrs. Vincent Kelly and her daughter were lost; and at Lamaline, Thomas Lockyer died of injuries.

Because the underwater telegraph cables were cut or damaged, communication was severely limited. The radio-equipped SS *Portia* was able to pass on messages, and the depth of the tragedy began to register as people heard about the terrible damage and destruction, the narrow escapes, the acts of bravery, and the heartbreaking loss of loved ones. Roads were washed out and bridges torn away, buildings shattered like matchsticks, and scores of severely injured people were in desperate need of medical aid. Fifty village outports were devastated, Taylor's Bay being one of the hardest hit, with twelve of its fifteen houses destroyed. Though all communities were eventually rebuilt, effects were long-lasting, as the inshore fishery took almost seven years to recover from the devastation. Economically, the disaster, one of the greatest in Newfoundland's history, was catastrophic to the area affected. The damage was estimated at over one million dollars. But the hardy fishing families of the Lower Burin Peninsula proved they had a determined resilience and strength of human spirit. They soon began rebuilding and within a short time were back on their feet and looking forward to a bright new future.

1931 A LETHAL BLAST DESTROYS THE *VIKING*

Most disasters at sea occur as a result of overwhelming weather conditions, usually storms or blizzards of lethal proportion. But for a ship lying quietly at sea to suddenly blow literally sky-high is a rare occurrence indeed. Yet that is exactly what happened to the *Viking*, a small Newfoundland sealing vessel.

The *Viking*, at 276 tons, was the smallest of the Bowring Brothers' fleet of Newfoundland sealing ships. But its size belied the experience and toughness it earned plying its trade for almost thirty years among the freezing waters and shifting ice off coastal

Survivors of the Viking *explosion, 1931*

Newfoundland. The ship was fully capable of carrying a full crew of 276, but for economic reasons, it took only 147 men for the 1931 sealing season, including several engineers and firefighters. Three American moviemakers were also aboard the *Viking* that fateful spring evening, as were two lads who were discovered stowed away on board. The *Viking*'s owners were proud of their fleet and of their safety record of fifty-two years without a loss of life. That was about to change.

On the quiet and calm Sunday evening of March 15, the *Viking* was lying snug and comfortable among the pack ice about eight miles south of tiny Horse Island, home to about thirty-eight families. On board, many of the crew were going about their evening duties, while others were relaxing in their bunks, sitting around chatting, or perhaps playing cards. The ship would be lying at anchor all night, so in the morning one of the first duties of the crew would be to free the ship from the frozen ice using blasting powder that had been stored away very carefully on board. The powder was being taken out and prepared during the evening, and it was during this activity that tragedy struck. At about nine o'clock, a terrific blast occurred, devastating the stern and setting the vessel on fire. It was never determined what caused the powder magazine to blow up, as all those who were close to the room perished. Perhaps an electrical wire shorted causing a spark, or an oil lantern had fallen over. About twenty of those aboard were killed outright while the rest of the crew fled onto the pack ice to escape the flames that were quickly destroying their vessel. The stern section of the vessel was blown clear of the ship and floated away, carrying three of the crew.

The nearest inhabited land was the Horse Islands, and the stunned survivors—some with severe injuries, including burns, broken bones, and lacerations—set out immediately for the tiny island outpost eight long miles away. Hampered greatly by the rough, shifting pack ice, a group of fifty finally arrived at the Horse Islands on Monday night, almost twenty-four hours after the explosion occurred, exhausted almost to the point of incoherence. By Tuesday night, a total of 118 survivors had reached the small settlement. Several other sealing ships, including the *Sagona*, *Beothic*, *Imogene*, and *Eagle*, scoured the area surrounding the explosion, hoping to come across survivors, or at least to recover bodies. The *Beothic* was successful in coming across three of the

Floating stern wreckage of the Viking, *1931*

Viking's crew huddled in a dory, cold, tired, and hungry, but with no major injuries. The *Sagona* came across the ship's stern, still afloat and with three much-relieved crewmen still aboard. Of the three American filmmakers on board the *Viking*, only one, Harry Sargeant of New York, survived. Varrick Frissel and A. E. Penrod, both from New York, perished.

Meanwhile, back on the tiny Horse Islands, survivors learned that it would be three to four days before any relief ship from the mainland would be able to get through. With the winter supplies of foodstuffs and medicine almost depleted, and no proper medical care for the many seriously injured sealers, the islanders were severely taxed, but still willing to give their all to help those suffering. Eventually a few of the rescue ships were able to get within three miles of the islands and sent medical aid. The *Sedona* sent in extra food and urged those who were physically able to walk to make their way out to the waiting ships.

The final death toll in the *Viking* disaster was 27 souls, while 126 individuals were saved. The bodies of most of those missing were never recovered. It was the first major incident involving sealers since the *Newfoundland* and *Southern Cross* tragedies of 1914, in which over two hundred and fifty men were lost in two separate disasters occurring on the same day.

1936 THE MOOSE RIVER GOLD MINE DISASTER INAUGURATES THE RADIO AGE

Although a disaster often involves a large loss of life, the number of victims cannot be the only form of measure. Trauma to the community, both economic and emotional, can also determine the immensity of any disaster. The Moose River gold mine incident is an example of this kind of disaster. Though only three people were involved in the event, and just one perished, the Canadian Press voted the incident Canada's top radio news story of the first half of the twentieth century. The high profiles of the trapped men and the media frenzy gave the story global exposure. Thanks to the work of the CBC's Frank Willis, news reports of the unfolding disaster were sent around the globe on a twenty-four-hour basis.

Gold mining in the little town of Moose River flourished from about 1890 to 1910, when the industry went into a decline and the mines were abandoned. The mine opened again in 1936 with renewed hopes of employment and prosperity for the town. Unheeded was the fact that the mine would be unsafe because the ore was being removed from the rock pillars that provided support from cave-ins. It all began on Sunday, April 12, 1936, less than two

Rescuers dig adjacent to the collapsed mineshaft, 1936

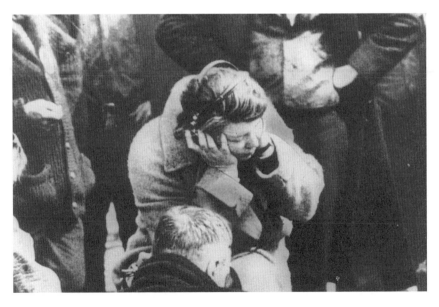

David E. Robertson's wife (name unknown) listening for sounds from her trapped husband, 1936

months after the mine reopened. On that day, two of the mine's owners decided to conduct an inspection. Dr. David E. Robertson and Herman Russell Magill were returning to the surface along with Alfred Scadding, the mine's timekeeper, when, about 140 feet from the surface, the mine shaft collapsed.

Timbers shattered as the earth caved in around the three men. When the tremors, noise, and dust finally stopped, they found themselves in a tiny space barely large enough for three persons. One large timber lay across the shaft, the only barrier preventing tons of rock from dropping on the trapped men. The cold and dampness began working on the men immediately, and the fight for survival was on.

Rescue workers were quickly on the scene and efforts were made to reach the men by using the adjacent Archibald and Meagher shafts. This didn't work, as these shaft walls proved to be too unstable for rescue attempts.

Meanwhile, the trapped men were trying to fight off the seeping cold and water. They were getting weak fast. As word of the unfolding disaster spread, newspaper reporters from all over the province poured into the area. Rescuers from several other mines were debating what steps were to be taken, but no one seemed to know the tunnel layout well enough to formulate a plan. Eventually, a Mr. Gladium was found who knew the mine workings. Heavy machines such as cranes and drills were brought in, but the road to the mine was becoming a quagmire and the mine site itself was very unstable. The Nova Scotia Department of Highways worked around the clock to repair the roadway as scores of rescuers and reporters poured in. Every building, shed, or scrap of shelter was used to house the growing throngs. Extra Mounties were called in to keep order.

Listening for signs of life, 1936

Survivors surrounded by rescue workers, 1936

The situation for the trapped men grew more serious. Magill contracted pneumonia and died a week into the cave-in, and the other two men were weakening fast. Many rescuers were losing hope that anyone would be found alive. An experienced driller from Springhill, Billy Bell, offered to set up his drill to find the men, but was turned down. Eventually Bell was given permission, and by April 18 he reached the area where they thought the trapped men would be. A whistling sound was sent through the pipe at intervals, finally attracting the attention of the trapped men who signalled back by tapping a pipe. Food, water, and fresh air were sent down until the men were finally brought out on April 23, having been trapped for eleven days.

Frank Willis of the CBC had arrived on the site on April 20, had quickly set up his equipment, and immediately began sending out a report every half-hour for the next fifty-six hours. Willis's reports were picked up around the world and drew more than a hundred million listeners. The coverage of the Moose River disaster had become the first truly global live radio event, and would herald the future of radio broadcasting. Interestingly, twenty-two years later, in covering another mining disaster (in Springhill), live television would come into its own as a worldwide media tool.

Over 350 rescue workers were honoured for their rescue efforts at Moose River, and today a small cairn, park, and museum mark the site where the drillers finally succeeded in reaching the trapped men.

1942 THE FERRY *CARIBOU* IS TORPEDOED

World War II affected civilian populations more than any other conflict in history. All of Europe was a battleground and millions of innocent people died. On the home front, Canadians felt safe and isolated from the fighting and carnage, even on the East Coast where the pivotal Battle of the Atlantic was raging. German U-boats were decimating Allied shipping efforts and preying on troop and supply convoys. Many ships in the merchant marine fleet had already been sunk by 1942, as had several warships. But because Canadian shores had not been attacked or invaded, most people felt that the civilian population would be safe until war's end.

St. John's and Halifax were the principal hubs of military activity on the East Coast, with convoys coming and going from these ports on a regular basis. As such, they were a fertile ground for the German "wolf packs." No one ever suspected that an innocent passenger ferry would be singled out and mercilessly torpedoed with no regard for passengers, civilian or otherwise. But that is what happened one cold October night in 1942.

The SS *Caribou*, built in the Netherlands in 1925, worked the Sydney–Port aux Basque ferry route for seventeen years, its schedule tying in with that of the famed "Newfie Bullet" passenger train. At 2,222 tons, the *Caribou* was 266 feet long and over 41 feet wide. Built to carry up to three hundred passengers and more than a thousand tons of cargo, it was a well-appointed and comfortable ship that served its public and its owners, the Newfoundland Railway, extremely well.

Ben Tavnor, captain of the SS Caribou, *1940s*

SS Caribou, *c.1940*

On October 14, 1942, the SS *Caribou*, captained by Ben Tavnor, left its Sydney berth at around 8:00 PM for the hundred-mile crossing to Port aux Basques. Its escort was to be the Royal Canadian Navy minesweeper, *Grandmere*. Since there was known U-boat activity in the area, the two ships would take a zigzag pattern. The unarmed *Caribou* would also sail under blackout conditions and carry extra lifeboats and life-saving equipment, as per wartime regulations. Aboard the ship that night were 206 passengers, including both civilians and service personnel. Using military procedure, the *Grandmere* followed the ferry at about a quarter-mile distance. The minesweeper was not equipped with radar and had only a short-range asdic (sonar), thus limiting its submarine detection capabilities greatly.

At around 3:00 AM, the *Caribou* was about twenty-five miles from Port aux Basques, nearing the end of a routine trip. Most of the off-duty crew and passengers were asleep. All was quiet. Unfortunately for the ferry and unknown to its escort, the German sub U-69 was cruising the surface, recharging its batteries, when it spotted the two ships. Unseen, it moved to an ideal firing position, targeting the starboard side of the *Caribou*. At about 3:30 AM, a well-aimed, high-explosive torpedo ripped through the ferry's starboard side and exploded near the engine, blowing up the boilers and causing tremendous damage. Many of the crew and passengers in that area were killed outright as the ship settled down, its sinking inevitable. Passengers raced for the lifeboats in panic, knowing they had only a few minutes, but the crew had difficulty swinging out the lifeboats amidst the pandemonium. The vessel went down within four minutes, many on board scrambling and jumping off the decks into the frigid waters, scores without lifejackets. Grabbing debris or whatever could hold them afloat,

The SS Caribou *and its crew, 1940s*

the desperate survivors could only hang on until their naval escort could pick them up. On seeing the explosion, the *Grandmere* spotted the sub and made chase.

But the U-69 dove quickly, evading the minesweeper. It was eventually learned that the skipper of the sub took refuge where he thought it would be safest, which was directly below the hapless group of survivors. The skipper knew that the escort would probably not fire depth charges among those still in the water. A short time later, the killer sub was able to slip away undetected. The captain of the minesweeper had followed correct military procedure in trying to find the enemy before helping survivors. He could not put his own ship in jeopardy. Eventually, 103 survivors were taken on board, two of whom died in hospital. Among the 136 men, women, and children who died in the tragedy were the captain of the *Caribou* and his two sons. One of the effects of the disaster was to harden the resolve of the Canadian military in combating the U-boat threat. Eventually, with improved sonar and radar capabilities, the dreaded submarines became less of a menace. Whether the U-boat's decision to sink a defenceless ship was a justified wartime act or cowardly act of murder has been debated ever since the tragedy. Many have said that because the boat was a civilian—and not military—vessel, was not armed, and took no part in wartime activities, the sinking was an unjustified act of murder. Others point out that although the *Caribou* was not a troop carrier, it sometimes carried servicemen on leave, both in and out of uniform.

1942 THE *TRUXTUN* AND *POLLUX* WRECKED AT LAWN POINT

THE WRECK

In February 1942, the US naval vessels the USS *Truxtun*, USS *Pollux*, and USS *Wilkes* were on their way to the US naval compound in Argentia, Newfoundland, when disaster struck. The cold February weather, unpleasant at the best of times, did not cooperate with the three warships when they ran into a heavy gale off the coast of the Burin Peninsula. Sleet and snow had reduced visibility to less than fifty yards. Combined with the unfamiliar rocky shoreline, this proved to be too much for the small flotilla, and on February 18, 1942, all three ships ran aground on the treacherous rocks off Lawn Point. The *Wilkes*, with a lot of tense manoeuvring, managed to free itself.

The *Truxtun* and *Pollux* were not so fortunate, both grounding hard and fast onto the granite boulders. The sterns of both ships had swung so that they were broadside to the incessant crashing

The USS Truxtun *in better times*

waves. The ships were flooding quickly, and the sharp rocks had smashed a hole through the *Truxtun*'s fuel tank. Thick oil soon spread everywhere around the ship, crashing with the seawater over the decks. The captains ordered all the crewmembers to come on deck with blankets, and to take shelter on deckhouses, galley decks, or wherever they could. If they could stay sheltered from the bitter cold, sleet, and wind, they might last until rescuers arrived. The jagged granite rocks were backed by vertical cliff walls, and the howling wind and vicious waves slammed the doomed ships repeatedly across the rocks and against the cliffs. It was far too dangerous to launch any kind of lifeboat in the darkness, especially in such storm conditions. The two ships soon began to break up, their hull plating unable to withstand the relentless onslaught. Keel plates buckled and gashes were ripped through to the engine compartments. The ships were literally being torn apart, and the

The USS Pollux, *destined for a bitter fate*

decks were sinking lower, now becoming fully awash with each pounding wave. Men were being swept overboard, while others, in attempting to swim ashore, were pulled onto the deadly rocks and perished quickly.

THE RESCUE

Sunrise found the men barely hanging on and the two ships battered and ripped apart, but still managing to stay more or less upright. But now at least the men could see. A boulder-strewn beach was spotted a few hundred yards along the shore that was away from the raging surf. The survivors lowered lifeboats, and ropes and heaving lines were used to finally attach a line to shore. With each raft taking six to nine men, many from both ships were taken to the beach. But problems still remained. The tall, ice-covered cliffs behind the small stretch of beach on which the men were

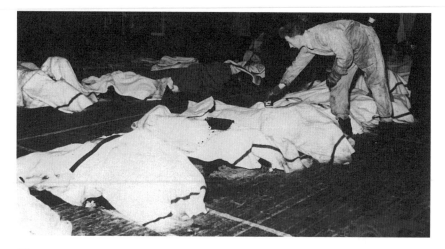

The temporary morgue, 1942

Rescue on the cliffs, 1942

marooned left no road, path, or foothold by which to get to the top. The survivors—wet, oil-covered, and slowly succumbing to hypothermia—would all soon perish unless help arrived.

As news of the disaster spread, help did arrive, albeit slowly at first. By midday several men from Lawn and the adjacent village of St. Lawrence appeared over the cliff top. Armed with plenty of rope and hooks, the rescuers hauled the stranded men up and over the cliff face. The rescuers started fires, and the survivors huddled closely, grateful to be alive. It was almost another twenty-four hours before the last man was hauled to safety, the rescuers by now bone-weary, wet, hungry, and tired. Eventually, more help arrived with blankets, food, and wagons.

The heroic efforts of the unselfish residents of Lawn and St. Lawrence were not in vain, as they saved the lives of 188 sailors from both ships. Sadly, 203 others succumbed to the elements while attempting to get ashore or while awaiting rescue. As tragic as the loss of the *Truxtun* and *Pollux* was, the disaster was also a study in human compassion, strength, and determination, as shown by the group of rescuers who gave their all in attempting to save as many as possible from certain death.

1942 AN INFERNO CONSUMES THE KNIGHTS OF COLUMBUS HOSTEL

THE HOSTEL

In 1942 Canada was still deeply immersed in World War II, and St. John's, Newfoundland, was still a major departure point for the troopships sailing overseas. Near and around St. John's were three army bases that swelled the city's population; the Americans had their base at Fort Pepperell and the Canadians had theirs at Gander and Torbay. Newfoundland was not yet confederated with Canada and so had its own Newfoundland Militia set up at Shamrock Field. From time to time there was intermingling among the three groups,

The Knights of Columbus Hostel, 1940s

especially at social events like the popular Saturday night "Barndance" at the Knights of Columbus Hostel. The hostel, a large, two-storey, wooden, L-shaped building, was being used as a serviceman's leave centre, supplying beds and a place for soldiers on leave to socialize.

The below-freezing evening of December 12, 1942, did not deter a crowd of four hundred from enjoying "Uncle Tim's Barndance" at the hostel. The event was so popular that each Saturday evening the dance was broadcast on the local radio station, many tuning in eagerly to listen to emcee Joe Murphy introduce such acts as local favourites Biddy O'Toole and Eddy Adams. It was the Christmas season and on this Saturday night the main dancehall was decorated and gaily festooned with streamers, bunting, and all kinds of other paper and cardboard ornaments. While many men and women were dancing and listening to the music in the main auditorium, others were playing ping-pong, listening to the jukebox, or just lounging in the smaller rec room off to the side of the canteen. Still others were sleeping upstairs in their bunks. In all, there were about five hundred people in the building that night, mostly servicemen.

THE FIRE

Just after 11:00 PM, Eddy Adams, having just been introduced by Joe Murphy, was breaking into his song when a chilling scream pierced the air, and a woman began screaming, "Fire! Fire!" People listening at home were shocked and even more perplexed when the radio suddenly went off the air. A moment later, back at the hostel, all the lights went out, leaving only the eerie orange glow of flames creeping along the ceiling. Then the pandemonium and panic kicked in, and the fatal rush to the exits began. The fire, later determined to have started in a bathroom storage cupboard in an open space over the auditorium, burned slowly, feeding on dry trusses and tarred rafters. All the oxygen was being consumed and replaced by deadly carbon monoxide. When the blaze finally broke through the ceiling of the auditorium and into the fresh oxygen and ceiling strewn with flammable paper bunting, the flames flared up wildly as if a firebomb had gone off. The fleeing crowd piled up at the exit doors, which, in a fatal error, were built to open inwards. Because of blackout regulations, most of the windows were boarded up. Other exit doors were nailed shut.

Streams of fire rained down on the revellers' heads from the burning decorations. Within minutes, people were collapsing from the toxic smoke, heat, and gas, and from the terrible burns they

The smoking ruins of the Knights of Columbus building, St. John's, 1942

were receiving. Several were saved by being hauled through the few windows that were smashed open. Many of those asleep in their bunks awoke to flame and smoke and managed to escape only by jumping through their second-floor windows. There were several acts of bravery, such as those of Constable Clarence Bartlett, who barged through the smoke and flames almost a half dozen times to carry out several people who otherwise would have perished. Hector Woolley and Gus Duggan, members of the Barndance troupe, died while trying to help others escape the flames. The pianist, Ted Gaudet, also fell victim to the stampeding crowd and was crushed to death. Teenager Doug Furneaux fought bravely and successfully to save others while people were dying around him. He managed to survive the inferno.

The hostel's bookkeeper, John St. John, tried to phone in the fire from his office in the hostel, but fire proved faster than the telephone operator. The bookkeeper's charred remains were found with his fingers still gripping the receiver. The fire department eventually arrived, about ten minutes after the start of the fire, but the building by then was just a mass of flames. The firefighters could only water down adjacent buildings, hoping to prevent the fire from spreading and destroying the whole city (St. John's had suffered several terrible fires in the past). It was three hours before the flames were finally controlled and extinguished.

All the next day, fire crews pried and sifted through the debris, trying to recover as many bodies as possible. The final tally was 99 dead and 107 injured, most suffering from severe burns. The grisly task of identifying the dead in the makeshift morgue took several days, as many of the corpses were burned beyond recognition. Even soldiers' dog tags were melted right into the scorched flesh. Throughout the following weeks, church bells tolled daily for the individual funerals of the nineteen civilians who died in the fire. A military funeral was held for the remaining eighty victims, a mixture of American, Canadian, and Newfoundland servicemen.

THE INVESTIGATION

Rumours of sabotage were rife, many believing the fire was deliberately set in the bathroom storage closet using rolls of toilet paper. One person claimed he saw a man close the closet doors, then run out of the building. On opening the closet doors, flames shot out from burning toilet paper. There was a rash of smaller fires throughout the city in the following weeks and one was reported to have been set using toilet paper. A subsequent investigation could not conclusively rule arson the cause, but what was discovered was the faulty state and construction design of the hostel. The building, which did not even have blueprints or specifications, seemed to ignore all safety features. Most crucial was the poor design of the

Funeral procession for fire victims, 1942

main auditorium, which did not exit directly to the outside. To get out of the building from the auditorium, people had to go down a hallway and cross another room before reaching the outside doors. Also, it was discovered that the emergency lighting was wired to the same panel as the regular lights; all went off together.

The fire was eventually ruled "of suspicious incendiary origin," meaning it might have been sabotage, but nothing could be confirmed, and the people of St. John's would never know for certain.

1943 THE *FLORA ALBERTA* SINKS

Nova Scotia fishermen have always plied their trade in a myriad of weather conditions. Freezing sleet can severely hamper speed and visibility, as can gales and sudden squalls. With the ever-changing storm patterns off Nova Scotia's turbulent coastline, the hardy and spirited sailors and fishermen generally know how to react to such weather conditions and manage to arrive safely at port—at least most of the time.

Fog can be deadly, as visibility is sometimes reduced to near zero. The captain must rely on a series of whistles and horn blasts, and perhaps radar if the ship is large enough. Mostly, though, the captain relies on his own instinct and pure luck. Sometimes luck is nowhere to be found, and that is usually when disaster strikes.

In 1943 the waters in Atlantic Canada abounded with boats and ships of all types. Because of the ongoing war, convoys consisting of transport vessels, troopships, and warships of all sizes were a common sight. Amidst all this naval activity, the small wooden fishing schooners went about their business all along the coastal areas of Nova Scotia. The *Flora Alberta*, out of the famed port of Lunenburg, was one such schooner. On the night of April 23, 1943, the *Flora Alberta*, captained by Gus Tanner and carrying a crew of twenty-seven men, was making its way in darkness through thick fog along the Nova Scotia coast, not too far from Halifax. Unbeknownst to Captain Tanner and his crew, the *Flora Alberta* was rapidly closing on a collision course with a military convoy. One of the ships in the convoy, the steamship *Fanad Head*, was bearing down on the little schooner, and the two ships actually saw each other for several seconds before they collided. Both ships took evasive action, the schooner desperately trying to alter course while the steamship threw its engines full astern. It was too late, as the *Fanad Head* slashed wickedly into the little fishing boat. The two-year-old schooner was cut clean in two and went down almost immediately. Most of the crew were asleep in their bunks when the collision occurred and stood little chance of survival. The *Flora Alberta* went down so fast that there was no time to launch even a single lifeboat.

The much larger *Fanad Head* suffered only minor damage and was soon able to dispatch three lifeboats to pick up survivors. But the schooner went down so quickly that only seven of its crew were rescued. Of the victims, only one body was ever recovered. It was assumed that others may have escaped from the sinking ship, but in the darkness they were not seen by their rescuers, and were lost. Captain Tanner, suffering from a broken arm, was among the seven rescued. The other survivors were Douglas, Garth, and John Reinhardt, all from Vogler's Cove; John Knickle from Blue Rocks; Walter Corkum from Pleasantville; and William Grandy from Garnish, Newfoundland. The victims left behind a total of at least forty children as well as fifteen grieving widows.

1944 A U-BOAT SINKS HMCS *VALLEYFIELD*

In May 1944 the dreaded U-boat wolf packs were still infiltrating Canada's coastal waters, river estuaries, and, in some cases, inner harbours. Thousands of tons of Allied shipping had already been sunk with hundreds of men lost. A great portion of Canada's naval fleet was thus used in convoy duty, protecting troop carriers and merchant marines from these deadly surprise attacks.

The HMCS *Valleyfield*, a river frigate of 1,445 tons, was built and launched in Quebec City in 1943. Commissioned for convoy runs, it had already served its country well, having completed a successful round trip overseas as a troopship escort.

HMCS Valleyfield *in port, c.1944*

Funeral for HMCS Valleyfield *victims*

On May 6, 1944, the *Valleyfield*, carrying a complement of 163 officers and men, was on the last leg home from its second convoy assignment. Four other naval ships accompanied the *Valleyfield* on that fateful night. All were heading for port at St. John's, Newfoundland. By 4:00 AM on May 7, the vessels were about fifty miles south of Cape Race and in sight of the Newfoundland coast. Radar and sonar detection, lethal to the U-boats, were made difficult and confusing by the presence of numerous icebergs in the area. However, the small flotilla felt there was no reason to suspect immediate danger. The officers and crews presumably just wanted to get back to port to enjoy some leave time. Little did anyone suspect that U-538 was lying in wait.

At 4:32 AM, Captain Eberhard Zimmermann ordered two Gnat torpedoes fired at the unsuspecting ships. The torpedoes were spotted, but too late. Alarms went off at once and battle station orders were given. Unfortunately, the U-boat's aim was true, and the *Valleyfield*, running astern of the other ships, took a direct hit on the port side. The boiler room was located in this area, and a tremendous explosion ensued, effectively breaking the spine of the doomed frigate. The seawater poured in, and in less than five minutes the *Valleyfield* had sunk. Those who were not killed outright by the blast now found themselves fighting for survival on the open sea. Others, who had no time to don lifejackets, grabbed on to anything that would float. Within minutes, the freezing water would begin taking its toll as the desperate men, most soaked in fuel oil, waited for one of the other ships to rescue them.

The other ships didn't immediately notice that the *Valleyfield* was missing, and when they did, they had to secure the area lest the U-boat was still waiting for another strike. This was accepted naval battle procedure, as lives aboard these ships were weighed against

Funeral procession for Valleyfield *victims, 1944*

those in the water. Sadly, many of those in the icy waters could not hang on long enough and quietly slipped beneath the waves. One hundred and twenty-five brave young sailors died that night in defence of their country. The commander of the *Valleyfield*, D. T. English, perished with his ship and all but two of his officers. Only thirty-six crewmen and two passengers survived. Each May, the Battle of the Atlantic is commemorated in Ottawa and in many other cities and towns across Canada in honour of the valiant crews of the *Valleyfield* and the scores of other Allied ships that were lost to the deadly U-boats.

1946 A DC-4 CRASHES AT STEPHENVILLE

The exact cause of an airplane crash often remains shrouded in mystery. Huge passenger airliners sometimes seem to just fall out of the sky with no communication from captain or crew. Accident investigators exhaust all efforts and yet fail to come up with any logical explanation. Passenger testimony is most unlikely because survivors are extremely rare. It can only be assumed, in some cases, that the crash was caused by a pilot navigation error.

In 1946 the airline travel industry was expanding at a rapid pace. Overseas routes were quite popular because many in the United States and Canada had family members stationed with the military in Germany. It was common for wives and children to fly over and spend some time with their loved ones. Douglas DC-4 liners were among the newest in airliner design and were used extensively on many overseas flights.

On October 3, 1946, American Overseas Airlines was ready to begin the Gander–Shannon leg of its New York–Berlin flight. The DC-4, huge by the standards of the time, set down on the runway at Harmon Field, a US military airfield near Stephenville, Newfoundland. Originally scheduled to pick up a fresh flight crew at Gander, the airliner had to be diverted to Harmon Field because of poor weather at the intended airport. Unable to change crews, the plane was delayed to allow the original flight crew sufficient rest before continuing the next leg across the Atlantic. During this period, the plane was serviced and its engines checked. All was in perfect order.

At 5:25 AM the plane was preparing for takeoff. Visibility was good and the ceiling was five thousand feet. Crosswinds were light at eight miles per hour. On board were thirty-nine people, including eight crewmembers. The captain, William R. Westerfield, was a veteran of countless crossings and had never had a mishap. Clearance was given and the DC-4 roared down the runway, lifting off in a seemingly routine procedure.

Approximately six minutes later, a huge fireball lit up a hillside seven miles away. Control tower and airport officials suspected the worst and immediately organized rescue teams. Converging on the burning wreckage, rescuers were appalled by what greeted them. The plane had plowed head-on into a hill about fifty feet below its crest. Completely unrecognizable, and shattered into thousands of pieces, the wreckage was engulfed in flames. It quickly became apparent that there would be no survivors. Only two of the victims were found away from the plane; the rest were consumed by the flames. The accident was the worst air crash up to that point in history. Although an exhaustive investigation was undertaken to determine the cause of the crash, no conclusive evidence was found. Assumptions eventually arose that the crash must have been caused by pilot error. The hill (Hare Mountain) was slightly fog-shrouded at the time. Perhaps the pilot miscalculated his circle pattern and flew in the opposite direction, unaware that he was below the hill summit. Or, as one person observed, "Maybe the pilot just forgot the mountain was there."

The following spring, the remaining wreckage was bulldozed into the ground and the covering soil landscaped into a memorial park, now called Crash Hill. A brass plaque and thirty-nine white crosses, one for each of the dead, now mark the site of the disaster.

PART THREE

1950 *to the*

Present

THE SECOND HALF of the twentieth century started off on a rather positive note, as for several years no major disasters were recorded. Modern firefighting equipment had, for the most part, eliminated the threat of devastating infernos in the region's cities and towns. Forest fires were still common, but controllable. Larger steel-hulled cargo boats and fishing vessels were built to withstand the fierce Atlantic gales—or so it was believed. Mining conditions were somewhat improved, using safer ventilation methods. Airliners routinely crossed the skies on their many transatlantic flights. Although living with the threat of a major disaster was ingrained in those who were involved in the fishing, sealing, and mining industries, it was all too easy to grow complacent, a dangerous sentiment especially when the forces of nature were involved.

The Springhill collieries were in continuous operation for almost a century, the only disaster being the heartbreaking explosion that occurred in 1891. But in 1956 and again in 1958, disaster struck, effectively putting an end to major coal-mining operations in the area. In 1992 the Westray coal mine near Plymouth, Nova Scotia, would experience a similar fate. In 1959 the fury of the volatile Atlantic took aim at the Escuminac fishing fleet in northeastern New Brunswick. Overnight, a sudden but fierce storm gripped the hapless fleet, destroying twenty-two fishing boats and taking the lives of thirty-five men.

Over the next forty years Atlantic storms struck again and again, claiming great seagoing cargo vessels as well as small fishing schooners. The *MV Gold Bond Conveyor*, the *Flare*, the *Cape Bonnie*, and the enormous and supposedly unsinkable oil rig the *Ocean Ranger*, all fell victim to the onslaught of raging seas.

The international airport at Gander, Newfoundland, experienced two disastrous air crashes, one of which saw all 256 on board perish. That 1985 crash was the region's worst air disaster up to that point. Only the 1998 Swissair crash off Peggys Cove was as keenly felt across the region.

Though rarely hit by large hurricanes, the Maritimes, notably Nova Scotia, experienced the wrath of Hurricane Juan in 2003. Though property damage was extensive, the death toll was minimal, perhaps a result of the solid design of the province's homes, built to withstand severe winter weather.

1956 ANOTHER MINE EXPLOSION ROCKS SPRINGHILL

Over a span of sixty-seven years, the small mining town of Springhill experienced three major mining disasters, in 1891, 1956, and 1958. The biggest, with the greatest loss of life, was the 1891 explosion that left 125 men dead. The 1958 "bump" was the most famous of the three, mostly because of the widespread media coverage and the dramatic rescue. The 1956 tragedy did not draw as much publicity, even though undaunted rescuers worked tirelessly for days freeing scores of trapped miners. World events, such as the invasion of Hungary by the Soviet Union and the subsequent refugee crisis, overshadowed the 1956 disaster, although the community of Springhill as a whole was traumatized by the knowledge that thirty-nine men would never again return to their loved ones.

Waiting for news, Springhill, 1956

THE ACCIDENT

The disaster occurred on November 1, 1956. On that day 127 men were deep in the mine working the No. 4 colliery. As is the case for most disasters, there was no indication or warning of what was to come.

Coal dust was always a concern in any coal mine; it could never be allowed to build up to dangerous levels, so cartloads of dust were continuously transported to the surface for disposal. It was during this procedure that a lethal combination of events occurred at the Springhill mine. First, as a small train of coal cars loaded with coal dust was being brought to the surface, the carts encountered a blast of fresh ventilation air coming down the No. 4 shaft. The fine coal dust soon began swirling and spreading through the shaft. Unfortunately, at the same time, some of the cars carrying the volatile dust uncoupled and began rolling back down into the mine. This was the worst thing that could happen, as the speeding, bouncing cars, combined with the ventilation air, were spreading the coal dust in heavy concentrations throughout the length of the shaft. All it would take now was one simple spark and the dust would ignite. Good fortune was not with the miners that day, as the dust-laden train sped out of control, going deeper and deeper into the mine. Suddenly, near the 5,400-foot level, the cars hit a bump on the track and derailed, jumping the track and running over a live electrical cable. The twenty-five-thousand-volt cable ripped, coming into contact with the iron wheels of the trolley, arcing violently, and spewing flame and sparks into the air. The dust in the air, by now mixed with enough oxygen to create perfect explosive conditions, ignited. A massive explosion ensued, blowing straight up the shaft, destroying everything in its path, including the bankhead buildings on the surface. Five men working in the pithead buildings were killed as a massive fireball shot two hundred feet into the air. Sirens on the surface soon began to wail, signalling to the townspeople that something serious had occurred at the mine site.

THE RESCUE MISSION

Crews of Draegermen—specially trained rescue teams who used self-contained breathing packs developed years before by Draeger, a German company—and barefaced miners were quickly organized. This would be the first time that the Draegermen's breathing

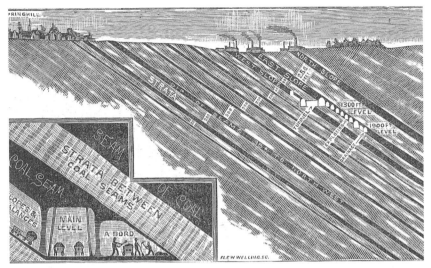

A map of the Springhill mine, 1956

Ambulances waiting for the injured, Springhill, 1956

equipment would be used to any great extent in the mine. At first, the rescuers feared the worst, as the shaft was damaged so badly that it seemed no miner could have survived. But the rescuers toiled steadfastly, slowly working their way through twisted steel, caved in walls, deadly pockets of gas, and shattered beams and pillars.

Damage at the surface, 1956

By November 2, thirteen men were confirmed dead. The rescuers continued, undaunted, and it was through the tireless efforts of these brave rescue crews that eighty-eight of the trapped miners were brought out alive. Luck was with one group of trapped miners who were able to tap into an air hose and breathe the life-saving air as methane gas swirled about them. On the surface, the fluctuations on the gas meter gauges indicated that the trapped men might still be alive. Rescue efforts were redoubled until the men were found. Nevertheless, the explosion killed thirty-nine miners on that tragic day. After several days, many fires were still burning in the mine. Because it was deemed too dangerous to recover the remaining bodies until the fires were out, the mine was sealed to let the fires burn up the remaining oxygen. After a couple of months had passed, the remaining victims were recovered and the mine reopened.

The miners and townspeople of Springhill had no choice but to put the tragedy behind them and try to go forward with new hope for a safe and prosperous future. But this was not to be, for within two years disaster would strike the small mining town once again, resulting in death and destruction so profound that the principal mining operations in Springhill would be brought to a permanent halt.

1958 THE BUMP ENDS COAL MINING IN SPRINGHILL

Coal miners working the deep collieries of the Cumberland deposits were well acquainted with tragedy and death. The dangers were an accepted fact of life for coal miners. Besides, a man could provide a good living for his family in this line of work. A healthy amount of luck might even assure that he would be around to see his kids grow up. Many of the men took a fatalistic approach, assuming that an accident would eventually happen; it was just a matter of time. In 1958, with the devastating 1956 explosion fresh in everyone's memory, the men were still nervous, not only about a possible gas or dust explosion, but about a major "bump," an instantaneous movement of two coal faces caused by extreme

Speaking to the media, Springhill, 1958

pressure. Similar to a small earthquake, these powerful rock shifts can cause considerable damage to mine workings, triggering falling rocks, sealing slopes, and, as pillars collapse, crushing or trapping anybody working the area. Small bumps were a common occurrence in the No. 1 and No. 2 collieries, something the miners were used to working with, even if they did worry about them. As the miners liked to say, "At least if you can hear the bump, well, you're still around, aren't you?"

THE BUMP

On October 23, 1958, 174 men were working the depths of the fourteen-thousand-foot No. 2 slope in one of the deepest collieries in the world. On the surface, the residents of Springhill—most related to the miners toiling down below—were just finishing up their evening meal. At 8:06 PM a ripple, then a strong tremor, ran through the town and the earth shook violently. The townspeople, jolted by a heart-stopping fear, knew what had happened. Many of the workers didn't. For those working in the bump zone, death was instantaneous, as floor and ceiling slammed together. In the surrounding areas, wall supports collapsed, ceilings caved in, rock walls burst, and tunnels were plugged solid.

THE RESCUE

Volunteer rescue crews and teams of trained Draegermen organized immediately while the families of the miners gathered at the pithead trying to comfort one another, but feeling only a growing despair. For a week, the rescuers toiled ceaselessly and unselfishly, bringing out survivors, many with severe injuries but grateful to be alive. The dead also were brought out, at least as many as the rescue parties were able to find. By the end of October, the Draeger teams were ready to concede that no one was left alive in the shattered mine. But they hadn't reckoned on the tenacity of the human spirit. On the seventh day of searching, desperate tapping on a pipe alerted the rescuers, and twelve men were found alive after seven days without food or water. All they had to sustain them was hope and prayer. Incredibly, on November 1, another six men were found alive, and their story of suffering in the face of death became one of legend. When it was all over, the final toll in the 1958 bump would be seventy-four men dead and ninety-nine rescued. The disaster also signalled the demise of large-scale coal mining operations in the town of Springhill.

Two survivors of the Springhill "bump"

THE MEDIA FRENZY

What set the 1958 Springhill disaster apart from that of 1956 was the extent of the news coverage generated by the disaster. In 1958 television was a new, rapidly growing medium. Though the news teams of many TV networks had been covering other local events on a regular basis, this would be the first time a breaking news story would be shown live across Canada and the United States. The arrival of reporters from all over Canada and the US launched an incredible media feeding frenzy, especially when the trapped survivors were brought up. As the dramatic TV reports were broadcast across North America, the public hung on to every word and picture of the desperate search for trapped miners. The reporters had unlimited access and conducted live interviews freely with rescuers, family members, mine officials, and the survivors themselves. Reporting was fair and the focus was not on who was to blame, but on the hope for more survivors.

There was a tremendous sense of unity among the community during the crisis: people were brought closer, not divided, by the disaster. Survivors were treated as absolute heroes. Some became national celebrities. When he reached the surface, reporters asked one of those rescued what the first thing he wanted was. He replied, "A 7-Up." He was later hired as a spokesman for the 7-Up soft drink company. When rescued, Maurice Ruddick, one of the trapped miners, made the statement, half in jest, "Give me a drink of water and I'll sing you a song." He immediately was dubbed "the singing miner" because of his supposed singing exploits while trapped. One of twenty-one nominees, Ruddick was chosen as the Canadian Citizen of the Year in 1958 by a newspaper poll conducted by the *Toronto Telegram*.

The media circus continued. Several of the rescued miners were invited to appear on the *Ed Sullivan Show*. The governor of Georgia at the time, Marvin Griffin, succeeded in exploiting the situation the most. Needing a boost for his lagging tourism trade, the avowed segregationist invited the rescued miners to a state-sponsored vacation in Georgia. Too late he discovered that one of the miners, Maurice Ruddick, was a black man. Ruddick and his wife spent their vacation segregated from the others. Even a picture of Griffin shaking hands with Ruddick conveniently disappeared. The miners, though, all agreed that it was the best vacation they ever had; for many of them, it was the only proper vacation they had ever taken.

CLOSURE

Realizing that many of the bodies of those lost would never be recovered, the mine owners decided to shut down the mine for good. Though a few attempts with smaller mines in the area went on for a time, the era of coal mining in Springhill was pretty much over. The collieries were flooded and eventually became a source of geothermal heat for the town. Today the mainstays of the town's economy include the Springhill Medium Security Prison, the Miners' Museum, and the Anne Murray Centre.

1959 DISASTER STRIKES THE ESCUMINAC FISHING FLEET

THE PEOPLE

The coastline of New Brunswick is well known for its pristine beaches, golden sand dunes, hidden coves, windswept capes, and raging surf thundering over treacherous rocks. The shoreline is also dotted with numerous tiny and picturesque fishing villages nestled in small coves and peppered with brightly coloured clapboard houses. In the summer of 1959, fishing boats of all sizes were moored in the gentle waters of community wharves as shrieking gulls wheeled overhead. On the southern shore of Miramichi Bay, facing the open waters of the mighty Gulf of St. Lawrence, lay the small and unassuming fishing villages of Baie Sainte-Anne, Bay du Vin, Hardwicke, and Escuminac, where the government wharf was located. The three-sided breakwater harbour, with its eighty-foot entrance, was well equipped and could handle up to a hundred thirty-five-foot boats. The well-maintained wharf was a gathering spot for fishermen along twenty miles of coastline.

The mainstay of the region's economy was, of course, commercial fishing. Young men followed their fathers and grandfathers into this traditional way of life. In fact, it was just about the only

Dignitaries gathered at Escuminac, 1959

line of steady work in the area. Boat owners and crewmembers knew that a good season, especially in Atlantic salmon or lobster, could be quite lucrative—that is, if they could handle the weary, backbreaking task of hauling in yards and yards of drift nets and lobster traps. If the catch was poor, then hardships would abound and the whole community would suffer. This had been the way of things for generations, the good taken with the bad.

That summer, the salmon were running in great numbers, and the season was shaping up to be one of the best in years. The month of June had seen excellent catches, and after a break of about two weeks to allow the salmon to go upriver to spawn, the catch resumed until its closing date of August 15. The morning of Friday, July 19, dawned bright and sunny. Seas were calm and no rough weather was in the immediate forecast. The crews spent the day preparing their boats for the afternoon departure. Traditional fishing procedures called for departure between 4:30 PM and 7:00 PM. This gave the fishermen time to set out their nets and ready up before darkness fell. The boat would then drift with the tide all night, the nets trailing behind. Each boat had a tiny cabin called a cuddy, which was just large enough to provide shelter for the crew. In the morning, the nets would be laboriously hauled in, which took several long hours, but hopefully produced a satisfactory catch.

More than fifty boats set out that Friday afternoon. In their optimism, many departed as early as four o'clock, eager to get the nets set in and, opting not to wait for supper, brought a lunch along instead. Those who listened to the Atlantic marine weather forecast before they left heard of some unsettled conditions, but no one was expecting anything too severe. The boats had no radios, so once at sea, the crews relied on instinct and on their own weather observation skills. Only at 8:45 PM that evening was a storm warning issued from Halifax. By this time, fifty-four boats were twelve miles out into the Gulf of St. Lawrence, their crews totally unaware that a killer storm, the most vicious in thirty-five years, was about to descend on the fleet with heartbreaking fury.

THE STORM

The storm overtook the flotilla around 11:00 PM, squall conditions quickly lashing the water into towering sixty-foot waves. Several boats headed to shore immediately, and managed to arrive safely. But the storm grew much worse, and the remaining boats and men fought for their lives. The heavy waves tore planking apart, ripped engines off their moorings, and flipped vessels completely over. Frantic hands bailed desperately as bilge pumps gave out under the onslaught of monstrous waves that flooded engine compartments, effectively disabling the boats and turning them over to the mercy of the raging sea. Crews thrashed helplessly in the churning waters, clutching at anything that would float. Twenty-two boats were shattered, swamped, and torn apart or lay wasted at the bottom of eighty feet of water.

In this hellish maelstrom of unbridled and merciless fury, thirty-six young men succumbed to the unrelenting force of nature. Those who managed to survive the night did so with a combination of prayer, hope, and desperate boating skills. Acts of heroism abounded. One boat, trying to ride out the storm and barely staying afloat, came across another vessel completely turned upside down. Jack Doucet and his two sons were hanging on to the wreckage, but were weakening fast as the frigid waters threatened fatal hypothermia. Getting close to the overturned boat, which could have slid to the bottom at any time, was a dangerous manoeuvre in such raging seas and ripping winds. If the rescue was poorly timed, both boats could be lost. The three were picked up and survived; most others were not as fortunate.

The fury went on unabated all night. On shore, an overnight vigil began as word spread about the unfolding tragedy. Relatives and friends of those still unaccounted for gathered together in growing apprehension while more and more wreckage was spotted, along with bodies of fishermen who fell victim to the vicious storm.

THE AFTERMATH

The RCMP and RCAF quickly set up bases to coordinate search and rescue operations in the air and at sea as soon as the storm tempered. Parties searched the shorelines for wreckage and pieces of identification.

The Red Cross set up headquarters to offer food and shelter to the growing number of people involved in the tragedy's aftermath. Several days after the storm passed, casualty figures started to

Escuminac monument

become clearer: thirteen were confirmed dead and nineteen were still missing. Eventually the death toll would be set at thirty-five. Almost 25 per cent of the fishermen who set out on July 19 never returned. Over 40 per cent of the fishing boats were sunk or destroyed. Left behind were seventy-six children and nineteen widows facing an uncertain future.

The economic impact was critical. The loss of boats, nets, and thousands of lobster traps was worth over 150,000 dollars. All along the coast, cottages, fishing gear, and many small boats were heavily damaged because breakwaters were unable to hold back the tempest. To help ease the hardship, the New Brunswick Fisherman's Disaster Fund was organized. Money poured in from all parts of Canada, and within several days 150,000 dollars had been collected and tons of food were being sent to the families of those who had been lost. Especially generous was the mining town of Springhill, Nova Scotia—itself no stranger to tragedy.

The local economy suffered a major setback, but despite the sorrow of losing so many loved ones, the rugged toughness and determined resilience of the people ensured that the devastating effects of the catastrophe could and would be overcome.

1967 WINTER STORM SINKS THREE SHIPS

The waters off the Atlantic coast of Canada can be fraught with danger at the best of times, but the winter months are especially perilous. Sudden storms are common, as are severe weather systems that can easily last a week, putting in jeopardy every ship that dares challenge the Atlantic.

In February 1967, a raging storm lasting almost seven days assaulted the coast and fishing grounds of Atlantic Canada. Most ships headed for home or made for the nearest sheltering harbour

The Cape Bonnie *founders in heavy seas, 1967*

to wait out the storm. A few other ships were able to limp into port, their crews feeling that luck was their guide. Three ships never made it home, with a total of thirty-five men lost to the icy ocean depths.

The *Cape Bonnie* was a 152-foot, 400-ton, steel-hulled trawler on its way back from a successful fishing trip to Brown's Bank. In its hold was over thirty tons of fish. Early in the morning of February 21, the *Bonnie* grounded on the Woody Island rocks, a treacherous piece of shoreline eighteen miles from Halifax and less than a mile from shore.

Ground fast with its port side listing into the raging hundred-mile-per-hour winds and thunderous waves, the hull of the doomed ship quickly filled with water, forcing the crew to abandon it immediately. Unfortunately, the lifeboats and the sailors' light clothing were no match for the freezing snow and sleet. Even the rescue helicopters sent out had returned, as the storm was simply too overpowering. Other boats and coast guard vessels managed to reach the *Cape Bonnie*, but by then hope for finding survivors was fading—it was estimated that a person could last no longer than five minutes in the face of such a frigid gale. Fourteen bodies were ultimately recovered, and after another day of searching, the search was terminated.

The *Iceland II* was a ninety-one-foot stern trawler out of Souris, PEI. When the storm struck, the *Iceland II* was fishing the Banquereau Banks off the southeastern shore of Nova Scotia with two other ships. The three ships headed to safety at Louisbourg and Mulgrave, but somewhere along the way the *Iceland II* blew off course and struck the treacherous rocks of Cape Forchu. The wreck was only discovered two days later, too late to save any of the crew. An empty dory and life rafts were found washed up on the rocks, and it was assumed all eight on board perished.

While the search for the *Iceland II* was going on, the *Pollie and Robbie* was reported overdue, having last reported off Cape Race several days earlier. Carrying a crew of seven, the *Pollie and Robbie* was discovered on February 28, when parts of a wheel-house bearing the ship's marking were found near Cape Race. It became apparent that the doomed ship had broken up during the same killer storm that also claimed the *Cape Bonnie* and *Iceland II*. Another ship, the *Maureen and Michael*, a schooner with a crew of eight, was also caught in the storm and foundered help-lessly. But just as the ship, completely at the mercy of the raging seas, was ready to go under, it was spotted by rescuers and all aboard were saved.

1967 A CZECHOSLOVAK AIR CRASH IN GANDER

Gander, Newfoundland, has for decades hosted airplanes from all over the world. Used as a sort of pit stop for aircraft flying from Europe, Gander has always been an important gateway to North America. The Gander International Airport can still boast one of the longest runways in all of Canada, and planes of all sizes land here for refuelling, crew changes, servicing, and connecting flights.

On the evening of September 5, 1967, several flights were arriving and departing smoothly, the highly competent traffic controllers busy with their night duties. Shortly after midnight, an Ilyushin IL-18 touched down smoothly on runway 32. The Russian-built turboprop, owned by Czechoslovakia State Airlines, had just finished the Shannon leg of a flight from Prague to Havana, Cuba. At Gander, the two-million-dollar, four-engine aircraft would be refuelled and serviced before taking off for its final leg with a fresh flight crew. At 2:40 AM the airliner was ready to roll down runway 14 with its 64 passengers and 5 crewmembers. The captain reported liftoff, but for some reason could not gain altitude. Evidently the pilot tried to make a soft descent and land the plane on its belly in a bog a mile from the runway. If he had been successful, many more lives might have been saved, but a CN railway line lying in a slight depression cut across the airplane's path. As the plane touched down, skidding wildly, it hooked and tore up a section of tracks, poles, and lines. Cartwheeling, the plane broke up quickly, its wings shearing off and its fuselage breaking into several large sections. Within a few seconds, 6,100 gallons of jet fuel ignited and everything was aflame.

Thirty-two died at the crash scene and three more died later in hospital. It was fortunate that many of those who lived through the ordeal were thrown from the plane when it broke up, being ejected away from the fire. The fact that the bog was extremely soft ground, thereby cushioning the impact, also aided those who survived. Rescue and recovery personnel were alerted immediately. Helicopter pilot Austin Garrett flew back and forth for six hours, bringing the wounded and dead out. The chopper wasn't equipped for night flying, so Garrett was guided to the scene only by the crash fires, landing by rescue workers' flashlights. By 10:30 that morning, all the injured and dead had been brought out. The veteran pilot was later honoured for saving so many lives. The fact that there were thirty-four survivors was also due to the efficient and prompt medical treatment by the staff of James Paton Memorial Hospital, both at the crash site and at the hospital. Inevitably, some of these survivors suffered terrible burns and other critical injuries.

So how could a plane, only six months old and in excellent mechanical condition, with a fresh flight crew and in good weather conditions, go down so quickly? There was nothing indicating a fire or explosion on board and no fuel leaks. Icing could not be a factor in September. Everything seemed normal. The final accident investigating report stated the cause was "undetermined." One could only speculate about pilot error. Many pilots take off on visual rules at night, if the sky is clear and the moon is out. Otherwise instruments are used. The night of September 5 was calm and dark with no moon visible. It may be argued that the pilot did not use his artificial horizon instruments enough, opting for a visual takeoff because the weather conditions were so good. Past the runway there were no visual references such as lights or buildings to indicate height. All that is known for sure is that a modern airliner took off and within seconds made a shallow decent into the ground, killing thirty-five of the sixty-nine souls aboard. Eighteen years later, a similar accident on takeoff at Gander would take the lives of every passenger.

1977 MYSTERIOUS ARSON AT THE SAINT JOHN JAIL

In 1977 the city lock-up in Saint John, New Brunswick, was located inside City Hall and, ironically, directly over a bank. On the night of June 21, a devastating fire broke out inside the jail, where twenty-seven men were being detained, mostly for minor offences. Twenty-one of the prisoners died, all overcome by thick toxic smoke.

Earlier in the day the jail had held twenty-two more prisoners temporarily moved from the provincial jail a short distance away. All but two were moved back to the provincial jail later in the day. Still, enough remained behind to warrant two extra guards. Many of the prisoners were young men guilty of misdemeanours no greater than underage drinking or disturbing the peace. Most were to be let out the next morning.

On occasion detainees at the jail had to be subdued if they became violent or hysterical, for which purpose the jail had a padded cell. The prisoner was usually searched thoroughly for any contraband: belts, laces, and matches were confiscated before he was put in the cell, which was also soundproofed for obvious reasons. Once the prisoner calmed down, he would be put in one of the regular cells, none of which had sprinkler systems.

Saint John Jail after 1978 renovations

On the night of June 21, a young man was brought in for creating a disturbance. John Kenney, no stranger to the lock-up, was in an agitated state and had already assaulted a police officer. So into the padded cell he went, after being searched and having all his cigarettes and matches confiscated—or so the police assumed.

A short while later, John Doiron, a seventeen-year-old locked up for underage drinking, smelled smoke and started banging on the cell window to attract the guards' attention, then grabbed his jacket, soaked it with water, and covered his face. As the smoke grew worse, the guards opened the door to the padded solitary confinement cell. As the fresh oxygen rushed in, an explosion ripped the cell door off its hinges. Thick black smoke began billowing throughout the cellblock. As Doiron described it, "Everyone was panicking. The prisoners were coughing and choking and yelling for the guards to unlock the doors." The guards had only one set of keys and had a hard time opening the steel doors because the heat was jamming the locks. Eventually the locks had to be cut with an acetylene torch, but it was too late for most of the prisoners. The 240 pounds of burning polyethylene foam from the padded cell released deadly cyanide compounds and poisonous carbon monoxide gas. Still locked in their cells, the prisoners never stood a chance. All of the dead were asphyxiated, not burned. Seven of the detainees were brought to hospital, where one died. When the explosion occurred, Kenney crawled into a small space in a corner. His face was only about eight inches from the floor, but he was able to breathe cleaner air. He and Doiron were among the fortunate six who survived. Six police officers were also injured in the fire, as was one firefighter.

It was determined that the fire in the padded cell could only have been started deliberately and with an open flame. Attention quickly focused on John Kenney, who adamantly denied starting any fire, arguing that all his matches had been taken from him when he was put in the cell. Although a book of matches was found in Kenney's pocket the next day, none of them had been used. Kenney was eventually convicted even though there was no concrete proof that he set any fire. The court reasoned that he was the only person in the cell and the fire started in that cell, so he must have started the fire. Found guilty of manslaughter, Kenney was sentenced to five and a half years in prison.

A public inquiry into the tragedy released its report in February 1978. It recommended discontinuing padded cells until fireproof materials were available, installing a sprinkler system, having duplicate cell keys available at all times, and training guards and police officers in fire prevention and fire emergencies.

1982 THE *OCEAN RANGER* DRILLING RIG FOUNDERS IN A STORM

THE RIG

The *Ocean Ranger*, a $124-million behemoth, was the pride of the offshore oil industry. The massive semi-submersible oil-drilling platform was the largest of its time and was considered, with its sophisticated ballast system and state-of-the-art control room, to be the most modern of its kind. Venturing into waters considered too dangerous for lesser rigs, the crews of the *Ranger* confidently and successfully took on jobs in several different venues, from the Bering Sea to offshore Ireland. The rig was, in fact, considered unsinkable. So sure was its crew of its invincibility that emergency safety and evacuation drills became lax and proper training was not completed. Tragically, this overconfidence would play a major part in the downfall of the *Ocean Ranger*.

Built by the Mitsubishi Company in Japan in 1976, by 1980 the rig was under contract to Mobil Oil Canada. In November of that year it was taken to the Hibernia Oilfield on the Grand Banks of Newfoundland, about 200 miles east of St. John's. Over the next fourteen months, the huge workhorse served its crews faithfully with no major problems, coexisting quite well with the often volatile North Atlantic.

THE STORM

On February 14, 1982, the rotation crew on the *Ranger* numbered eighty-four men, including fifteen Americans. The rest were Canadians—thirteen from Alberta, Ontario, and Quebec, and the majority, fifty-six men, from Newfoundland. It being Valentine's Day, it's probable that many of the men were thinking of their

The Ocean Ranger *one week before its sinking, 1982*

loved ones back on land. Perhaps others were monitoring the weather and a fast-approaching storm coming up from the south of Newfoundland.

By 6:00 PM, the storm raged over the *Ocean Ranger*, with towering hundred-foot seas and ninety-knot winds. Though buffeted continuously by the raging wind and breaking waves, the men were not overly concerned and were prepared to patiently wait out the storm, as they had at other times. But the storm's "rogue waves" were reaching and crashing on to the rig's high upper deck. As a precaution, the crew decided to try and detach the drilling platform from the main deck but were unable to do so. Around 7:00 PM, an especially large wave broke over the ballast control room, smashing a porthole window. The amount of water let in by the wave shorted out some sensitive electrical equipment that monitored the ballast balance. Some flooding occurred, causing a list of about ten degrees. Several shorted out relays were quickly removed, dried, and reinserted. Again they shorted out. The listing remained.

There were no written instructions on how to deal with ballast emergencies, just advice passed on from crew to crew by word of mouth. It was decided to even the balance by pumping water out of one ballast tank. Here, the fatal mistake was made: instead of pumping water out of the flooded ballast, water was accidentally pumped in, increasing the list to a precarious fifteen degrees.

Around 1:00 AM, the *Ocean Ranger* radioed the shore base at St. John's requesting the supply ship to standby. Ten minutes later a frantic SOS was sent out, requesting help to get the crew off the rig because they were worried it might go over. At 1:30 AM, in their last radio message, the crew signalled that they were going to lifeboats. That was the last anyone heard from the *Ocean Ranger*. At 3:30 AM, search and rescue ships were stunned to watch the rig disappear from their radar screens.

RESCUE ATTEMPTS

In their panic, several of the crew got washed off the deck or were blown overboard by the tremendous winds. Several others, confused and fearful, simply leapt over the side into the frigid Atlantic

Empty lifeboat from the ill-fated Ocean Ranger

instead of getting into the lifeboats and soon perished. Even the lifeboats were no match for the raging storm: in the ninety-mile-per-hour gale, they just flipped over, dumping the desperate men into the freezing waters. There were not enough survival suits for everyone and those who wore them did not last much longer than the others. Those who attempted to stay afloat by swimming or hanging on to flotsam succumbed in moments.

Rescue ships and a helicopter arrived at the scene at around 2:00 AM. Men were spotted in the water and in a lifeboat, but the rescue ship and chopper could not manoeuvre close enough to pick the men up. Rescue lines were thrown and at one point the men in the raft made desperate lunges to grab the rope. They couldn't hang on, and the raft upset, throwing the terrified crewmen to their fate. Another large inflatable rescue raft was thrown out to the drowning victims, but by now overcome by the numbing cold, the hapless oilmen could not reach it in time. Grappling hooks and long poles were also tried, in hopes of grabbing a piece of clothing, but to no avail. To the anguish and heartbreak of their would-be rescuers, the doomed crewmen eventually disappeared forever into the icy depths of the Atlantic. At 3:38 PM the *Ocean Ranger* sank, following its men to a watery grave. All eighty-four crewmembers perished, though only twenty-two bodies were recovered.

THE ROYAL COMMISSION

The Canadian government immediately launched a full inquiry into the disaster. After an exhaustive two-year study of all aspects of the *Ocean Ranger* tragedy, the Royal Commission released its report on the sinking. In it the commission concluded that a number of factors combined to seal the fate of the drilling rig, including serious design flaws in its ballast structure. Perhaps more important was the conclusion that the crews were poorly trained in safety and emergency preparedness. The *Ocean Ranger* may well have survived if its ballast room operator had been better trained. As it was, even the senior operator had only completed half his training. The commission also noted that the survival gear was not adequate for the harsh Atlantic Ocean environment.

As a result of the inquiry, several new federal government regulations were implemented and monitoring boards were established to oversee the Canadian offshore oil industry. Proof of competency, stringent training requirements, and modernized and suitable life-saving equipment would all help ensure that a disaster as terrible as that which befell the *Ocean Ranger* not happen again.

1985 A GANDER AIR CRASH RAISES SUSPICIONS OF TERRORISM

By 1985 there was finally some agreement in the volatile Middle East, as the Camp David peace accord was drawn up. To enforce the accord, a multinational peacekeeping force was assigned to the Mount Sinai area on a rotating basis. Making up the American contingent were members of the 101st Airborne Division, known to most Americans as the legendary "Screaming Eagles." On December 11, having completed their tour of duty, 248 members of this elite unit boarded a civilian aircraft in Cairo, Egypt. Their final destination, Fort Campbell, Kentucky, would be reached via Cologne, Germany, and Gander, Newfoundland. The chartered Arrow Air DC-8 landed in Cologne for a brief crew change and servicing. At 11:20 PM on the evening of December 11, the plane departed on its next leg to Gander. Undoubtedly, most on board were thinking of their loved ones and how great it would be to be back home for Christmas. The DC-8 landed at Gander at 5:34 the next morning. While the plane was refuelling, the passengers had a chance to stretch their legs and get some fresh air. By 6:45 AM, all the soldiers and eight crewmembers were back on board, preparing to roll down the runway for the flight to Fort Campbell.

A minute later, something went horribly wrong. Though the plane lifted off, it was sluggish and unable to gain much altitude. Normally, as a plane reaches critical takeoff speed, enough lift is generated so that it can easily reach its intended path. In this case, something caused drag on the DC-8, preventing the airplane from gaining the necessary speed for proper lift. Finally, a low speed stall sealed the airliner's fate. Unable to recover, it made its fatal plunge to earth, plowing into a small hillside about one kilometre

Silent Witness, *the memorial to the victims of the crash*

from the end of the runway. As the airliner broke up, the fuel tanks ruptured and ignited. A giant fireball lit up the early morning sky, and the few who witnessed the crash held little hope for survivors. Sadly, they were right, as the crash killed all 256 on board, making it the worst air disaster ever to occur on Canadian soil.

Even before crash investigators arrived, there were conflicting theories about what caused the crash. Heavy icing on the wings seemed to be the most logical explanation, and a report by the Aviation Safety Board officially ruled that icing was indeed the likely cause of the disaster. Several members of the board did not fully agree with the ruling, insisting more investigation should have been done to verify whether it might have been sabotage. In fact, several eyewitnesses testified that they had seen an explosion before the plane hit the hillside. Several Islamic terrorist groups also claimed responsibility, but this was quickly ruled out by US authorities. Today, the investigation remains closed even though independent investigators have offered new theories suggesting that it may have been something other than heavy icing which caused the crash. In 1990 a memorial statue was unveiled at the crash site commemorating the victims, who died knowing that as peacekeepers they had truly done their part in making the world a safer place to live.

1992 AN EARLY MORNING EXPLOSION DESTROYS THE WESTRAY MINE

THE MINE
By 1992 there were few active coal mines left in Atlantic Canada. Petroleum-based fuels and nuclear-generated power had largely replaced the need for coal as a primary energy resource. Still, a few mines did operate, and one of these was the Westray mine in Plymouth, Nova Scotia. Owned by Toronto-based Curragh Resources, the mine boasted the latest in high-tech equipment. The owners set high production rates and the crews worked twenty-four hours a day, seven days a week, to meet heavy quotas.

Despite repeated complaints by many miners that the mine was unsafe, company officials insisted the mine was indeed safe. Most of the men were new to the job, not fully or properly trained, and not as familiar with methane gas as they should have been. On May 9, 1992, the inevitable occurred.

Marble monument located in the Westray disaster memorial park

FIRE AND EXPLOSION

At 5:15 AM that day, twenty-six men were working the night shift at Westray. Split into two work groups near the 4,200-foot level, the men were using one of the "continuous mining machines," a modern and popular device that enabled the miners to access and extract the coal with great efficiency. The coal faces contained many pockets of methane gas, which were set free as the work progressed. Unknown to the men was the accumulation of gas in ceiling pockets all along the tunnel roof. Suddenly a spark from the machinery ignited the methane in the ceiling. In seconds the fire spread along the tunnel ceiling. Miners who never had time to reach for their emergency air kits died quickly as the lethal by-product of carbon monoxide gas overtook them in seconds. It would not have mattered, because the fire, which soon reached the main slope, had stirred up the highly volatile coal dust. In a split second the dust exploded in a tremendous blast that reached all the way up to the surface, blowing the mine entrance building to bits. The explosion thundered through the north and south mains, where the twenty-six men were working. Death, for those who had not already succumbed to the carbon monoxide gas, was instantaneous. As in all coal dust explosions, the damage was severe. Just about anything in the path of the blast was completely destroyed, crumbled and twisted beyond recognition. Ceilings and walls caved in as timbers snapped and supports gave out. In a matter of less than a minute, twenty-six men died. The shattered mine was a complete ruin and would never again be reopened.

Rescue crews (Draegermen) worked desperately to get to the miners. The going was slow and dangerous, with deadly gas pockets everywhere. Fifteen bodies were recovered over the next four days and the search continued for another day or so, but the extent of damage suggested that it was unlikely anyone could have survived. The search was eventually called off, leaving eleven bodies still buried.

ACCUSATIONS

Questions were soon asked regarding the way the mine was run, in particular whether the mine's practices had been unsafe. Miners were coming forth with stories of company arrogance and "take it or leave it" attitudes. Over the years, several inquiries were held, reports filed, various lawsuits, appeals, and legal actions taken. There were accusations and counter-accusations, charges filed and charges dropped. But the bottom line is that no one was ever found legally responsible for the disaster. The families of the victims, those who suffered the most, were given relatively small pensions, allowances, or settlement payments, but never received closure.

1993 THE MV *GOLD BOND CONVEYOR* SINKS IN A "PERFECT STORM"

Today's giant supertankers and massive cargo ships ply the oceans around the world, ready to tackle any kind of sailing conditions. These tough boats are built to withstand just about anything that Mother Nature can throw at them. But every now and then a storm system will come along and make a mockery of our smug and overconfident attitudes. The *Ocean Ranger*, the *Flare*, and the *Andrea Gail* are just a few recent examples of ships that dared challenge a perfect storm, with consequences that were nothing short of disastrous and tragic. "The perfect storm" has become a popular phrase since Sebastian Junger published his book of that title in 1997; the book chronicles the exploits of the ill-fated *Andrea Gail*, a fishing boat from Gloucester, Massachusetts, that was lost off the coast of Nova Scotia in 1991.

In October 1993, a huge energy system that had its early development down in the warmer climes of Florida was pushing its way up the eastern seaboard, gathering strength as it approached Canadian waters. At this point, meteorologists, forecasters, and those in the know were calling the storm "once in a lifetime," "historic," and "an unprecedented event." Described as "a perfect storm" by many others, the system wreaked tremendous havoc as it raged northward along the East Coast, shutting down all vital transportation links, including most airports and train services. By the time the storm moved into Atlantic Canada, sixteen deaths on land had occurred, and the storm's viciousness and intensity were awesome. Although most boats would not dare venture out in such adverse weather conditions, at least one ship was caught off the coast of Sable Island.

FIRE AND EXPLOSION

The *Gold Bond Conveyor* was a behemoth of a bulk carrier with a length of about 530 feet. It was ocean-tough and built to withstand whatever the mighty Atlantic offered up. Apparently, though, its designers did not reckon on the "rogue waves" that are the trademark of so many East Coast storms. Waves from this particular storm were cresting up to sixty feet. The *Conveyor*, already deep in the water with its full load of gypsum, could not handle the giant waves and at 3:05 AM radioed that it had developed an eighteen-degree list to port, declaring its situation "dangerous." Rescue coordination centres picked up the message and immediately tasked aircraft and vessels in the vicinity to respond. Fifty minutes after its initial distress call, the *Gold Bond Conveyor* reported a twenty-three-degree list. Twenty-four minutes later, at 4:19 AM, the frantic radio operator declared a final mayday and announced the crew was abandoning ship.

Rescuers listening to this disheartening message knew what it meant. The waters at that time of year were frigid, and no one could last long on the open sea, not even in a lifeboat. Time was crucial. Nine minutes later, a search plane spotted the doomed cargo ship just as it rolled over and went down. The plane threw marker flares, but no lifeboats or survivors were seen. Eventually, twelve Canadian Forces aircraft and boats performed an extensive search for survivors, but none were found, and the entire crew of thirty-five was officially declared lost. Interestingly, the *Gold Bond Conveyor* was struck by a rogue wave in the same area where the famous *Andrea Gail* had gone down two years previous.

1998 THE *FLARE* BREAKS UP AT SEA

Today's huge carrier vessels are built to withstand the roughest of seas and carry on their trade in all kinds of weather conditions. Accidents rarely happen, and when one does, it is often the fault of the ship's owners in disregarding proper servicing procedures or of the skipper in neglecting to upgrade necessary emergency and life-saving equipment.

The *Flare*, launched in 1972, was a Japanese-built, Greek-owned bulk carrier designed for various ore or grain cargoes. At 16,398 tons, the *Flare* had a length of 590 feet, a breadth of 75 feet, and could reach, at service speed, 15.1 knots. The aft end of the ship contained all crew quarters, the wheelhouse, life-saving equipment, and engine rooms. The ship also contained nine watertight bulkheads, and its reinforced cargo holds could be used as extra ballast tanks when empty.

The *Flare* departed Rotterdam on January 16, 1998, after picking up eleven crewmembers in that city, bringing the total ship's company, including officers, to twenty-five, from four nationalities. It was the captain's first command on a bulk carrier of such size, although he had served as first mate on similar ships and as skipper on smaller carriers. Structural repairs that should have been done in port were not completed, so welding equipment and steel plating were brought on board before departure, for repairs to be made during the trip on several ballasts tanks. As a result of the incomplete repairs, the ship's ballast tanks were not filled to necessary levels at the start of the voyage.

The weather was terrible from January 1 onward. Seas reached heights of up to fifty-two feet and gale-strength winds blew almost continually, causing the boat to pitch heavily. Also, perhaps because of the low ballast, the carrier was subject to severe slamming and pounding on its fore end. The noise of the continual pounding and flexing of the hull was worrisome to some of the crew, preventing them from sleeping and eating. One crewmember was so concerned that he practised putting on warm gear as fast as possible, and kept his light on, just in case. These actions may very well have saved his life.

In spite of its problems, the *Flare* made headway, and by January 16 the ship was approximately forty-five miles southwest of the French islands of Saint-Pierre and Miquelon. At around four o'clock that morning an extra-loud bang could be heard from the forefront, along with an extreme shuddering and vibrating sensation, as the ship's hull flexed and whipped. About four hours later there was an even louder bang followed by even more intense whipping. The crew, located at the aft portion of the ship, rushed out as the general alarm sounded. When the men saw the state of things, many of them knew their fate was sealed. The *Flare* had broken completely in two, the fore section slowly drifting away from the aft.

The men tried to get at the motor-driven lifeboat on the starboard side but because the stern section was listing at almost a thirty-five-degree angle to starboard, they could not reach the lifeboat. Meanwhile, the port life raft had been lashed double to secure it during the rough voyage. In the total darkness, with the deck covered with slippery ice, sleet, oil, and snow, the panicking crew were not able to free the boat. As the captain was sending out a hurried mayday, another lifeboat was lost as it floated out of reach. The stern went down within thirty minutes of breaking in two, and the terrified crew, all in life jackets but wearing light clothing, barely had time to clear the sinking hull. Six crewmembers managed to climb on an overturned life raft and hung on for dear life. But it was not enough for two of this group who succumbed to the cold and slipped away. The other four on the raft managed to hang on and were eventually spotted and rescued, barely alive. Sadly, they were the only survivors of the crew of twenty-five. The fore section of the *Flare* finally sank four days later.

The mayday sent out by the doomed carrier was picked up as a very faint signal at the coast guard station in Stephenville, Newfoundland. Once the mayday was verified, search and rescue teams quickly went into action, sending out aircraft and helicopters and contacting any ships in the immediate area for help in the search. The four survivors on the lifeboat were soon spotted, picked up, and brought to a hospital on the island of Saint-Pierre. By 6:00 PM fourteen bodies had been recovered, and by 8:00 PM all the lifeboats and life rafts from the *Flare* were accounted for. The search was then scaled back, as it was determined that a person could not last much longer than two hours immersed in the frigid Atlantic waters. Airborne and marine search and rescue personnel spent more than ninety-nine hours on the mission.

In the aftermath of the sinking, the Transport Safety Board cited several contributing factors that led to the *Flare* disaster. The board's report found that the *Flare* had unrepaired structural damage as it left port in Rotterdam, and its ballast was insufficient and may not have been properly distributed. The extremely poor weather and rogue waves on the voyage across the Atlantic put further pressure on already existing fissure damage. The report also found that the ship was lacking in emergency preparedness. The *Flare*'s emergency radio beacon was not activated and no signal was ever received from the ship SART (search and rescue transponder).

Moreover, none of the six survival suits on board were used, possibly because survivors didn't know where they were stowed.

The *Flare* disaster shows us clearly that complacency can lead quickly to fatal and tragic consequences. In this case, lack of prompt attention to minor structural damage, as well as inattention to proper emergency equipment and procedure, led to the deaths of twenty-one men.

1998 SWISSAIR FLIGHT 111 CRASHES NEAR PEGGYS COVE

THE CRASH

At JFK International Airport, early in the evening of September 2, 1998, 229 people boarded a McDonnell Douglas MD-11 aircraft designated Swissair flight 111. Along with the 215 passengers were pilot Urs Zimmermann, co-pilot Stefan Low, and the flight attendant crew of twelve. The majority of the passengers were American, the rest mostly Swiss and French, plus a lone Canadian. Their planned destination was Geneva, but tragedy struck just short of an hour into the flight.

Fifty-seven minutes out of JFK, the airliner was approaching the coast of Nova Scotia and cruising smoothly at thirty-three thousand feet. The passengers were reading, relaxing, listening to music, and watching videos on the plane's entertainment system—nothing seemed amiss.

At 10:10 PM (Atlantic Standard Time) the pilots noticed a slight odour of smoke in the cabin. Thinking that the smoke was coming from the air conditioning system, the flight crew was not too worried until about four minutes later when the smoke grew visible and much stronger. The pilot, now extremely worried, requested a diversion landing. He suggested Boston, but air traffic controllers directed the plane to Halifax, about a hundred kilometres away. At 10:19, with the cockpit now filling rapidly with smoke, the flight crew began a rapid descent. First, as a landing precaution, the plane needed to dump fuel, but time was quickly running out. Heat and smoke were shutting down the all-important lighting and instrument systems, including autopilot. At 10:24, the crew declared an absolute emergency as systems continued to fail. A few minutes later, and still too far from Halifax, the pilot was fighting desperately for control of his aircraft and in pitch-black darkness. The flight crew had no way of directing the plane, either by instruments or manually.

At 10:31 time ran out as the plane, now completely out of control, hit the water at a speed of three hundred knots, at an angle of twenty degrees nose down, and almost upside down. With an impact force of 350 g-force, death would be instantaneous for all aboard. Recovery efforts indicated the plane was broken into approximately two million pieces.

RECOVERY AND INVESTIGATION

More than 350 investigators were involved in the aftermath. Poring over 98 per cent of the wreckage (2 per cent was never recovered) proved to be a slow and painstaking process that took four years and fifty-seven million dollars to complete. The investigation was hindered by a lack of recorded information. Although the airplane's flight recorder and cockpit voice recorder were both recovered, it was found that both had stopped at ten thousand feet, a full six minutes before the impact.

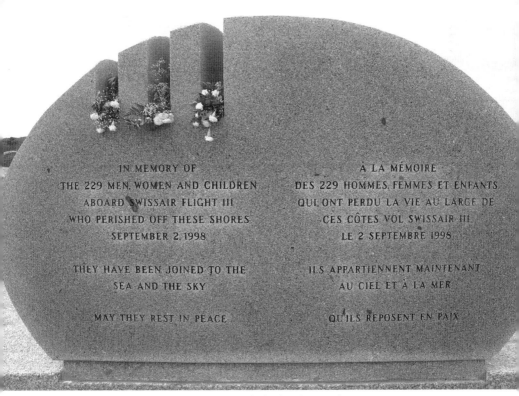

The Swissair monument at Whalesback Beach

In 2003 the Canadian Transportation Safety Board final report on the disaster indicated several factors as contributing to the tragedy. Wiring from the inflight audio-video system ignited flammable material, although exactly what caused the wires to overheat could not be precisely determined. Circuit breakers did not trip as the fire spread to other flammable materials. The flight crew became aware of the situation too late because no instruments indicated a fire, which had spread rapidly, knocking out all-important lighting in the cabin. Heat in the cockpit built to such an intensity that the ceiling actually began to melt. In such an environment, the flight crew could only fly blindly, and disaster was inevitable. Based on these findings, the TSB recommended that future planes have fireproof materials, improved fire detection and suppressant systems, and reliable flight data recorders. Although modern technologies such as these can make flying much safer that it has ever been, it is unfortunate that lives have to be lost before our mistakes are corrected.

The unidentified remains of several victims are buried at memorial sites near Bayswater and Blandford, communities that took an active role in recovery operations. Also at the Bayswater site is a memorial wall containing the names of the crash victims.

A second monument is located near Peggys Cove at Whalesback Beach. The memorials, designed by Richard Earle of Dartmouth, are elegant but modest, in keeping with family wishes. According to Mr. Earle, "the concept and placing of the design was to place the physical structure of the monuments behind the viewer, quietly concentrating attention on the accident site and the serene beauty of the St. Margaret's Bay area." Over six hundred family members gathered at the monument sites where the unveiling took place in September 1999.

2003 HURRICANE JUAN LASHES NOVA SCOTIA

THE UNEXPECTED STORM

Every year tropical storms and even hurricanes manage to roar ashore, usually in the southeastern states, where they wreak havoc before weakening and quickly dissipating. Some never reach land, but instead sweep up along the eastern seaboard before swinging back out into cooler water and rapidly weakening. It is not uncommon for coastal Nova Scotia to pick up the dying remnants of these storms. Above-normal tide surges, heavy rains, and extra-strong wind gusts are the norm in such storms. But full-blown hurricanes are quite rare and unexpected.

In fact, it had been well over a century since a storm of a major magnitude had hit Halifax, the last being a Category 3 hurricane in 1893 that sank several vessels and claimed twenty-five lives. But the hardy people of Atlantic Canada were much more used to winter blizzards, snowstorms, and freezing conditions.

On September 29, 2003, the Atlantic provinces were to experience the full extent of nature's fury as Juan, a powerful and fast-moving Class 2 hurricane, made landfall, slashing a 110-mile path through Nova Scotia, New Brunswick, and PEI. Juan was an extremely quick-forming storm, having gone from a small tropical depression south of Bermuda to a tropical storm in just six hours; twenty-four hours later, it had developed into a full-fledged Class 2 hurricane bearing down on mainland Nova Scotia. Halifax took the brunt of the storm, which came ashore just after midnight with sustained winds of 98 miles per hour and gusts up to 144 miles per hour.

The fury of the hurricane was awesome; it uprooted thousands of trees, ripped roofs off homes, and toppled power and telephone lines, knocking out electricity and communication. Deadly debris flew through the air, smashing cars and buildings. The deluge of rain, combined with the highest storm surge ever seen in Halifax Harbour, produced sixty-two-foot waves, causing heavy damage from extensive flooding along the historic waterfront district of Halifax. Juan, which had made landfall shortly after midnight on September 29, was downgraded to a tropical storm by 3:15 AM,

A satellite image of Hurricane Juan, 2003

just as it was reaching PEI, though winds were still sustained near sixty-two miles per hour with gusts up to eighty-seven miles per hour.

THE AFTERMATH

The widespread havoc wreaked by Hurricane Juan resulted in more than fourteen hundred applications for disaster relief, which eventually resulted in payouts of over twenty million dollars.

An unfortunate parking spot, 2003

Most people who experienced the great storm were surprised that only eight persons perished. Four were killed as a direct result of the storm's ferocity and four others were killed in the hurricane's aftermath. John Rossiter, a young Halifax paramedic, was killed when an uprooted tree crushed his ambulance. In Enfield, Nova Scotia, another man died when a vehicle was also crushed by a falling tree. Two fishermen from Caraquet drowned when their fishing boat capsized near Anticosti Island in the Gulf of St. Lawrence. And, as a result of using candles during the power outages, a woman and her two young daughters perished in a tragic house fire. One other person died while involved in relief work weeks after the storm.

Many believed that casualties were light only because of the rugged construction of Maritime homes, which are built to withstand harsh winters. Based on the assessed damage, Hurricane Juan is considered to be the most devastating hurricane to hit Atlantic Canada in modern times. In fact, the impact was so great that Juan, the storm's name, has officially been retired.

Sources
& Index

SELECTED BIBLIOGRAPHY

Bird, Will R. *These are the Maritimes.* Toronto: Ryerson Press, 1959.

Brown, Cassie. *A Winter's Tale: The Wreck of the Florizel.* Toronto: Doubleday, 1976.

Brown, Kingsley. "More Blood on the Coal." CBC Archives, CBC Newsmagazine, Oct. 26, 1958.

Collingridge, Shirley. "Ten Days in Hell: The 1936 Moose River Mine Disaster." shirleycollinridge.com/mooseriver.htm

Elliot, Norma. "Burning of St. John's, NFLD, 1892." Newfoundland Grand Banks Genealogy Site, December 2003. http://ngb.chebucto.org/articles/1892

Harrington, Michael. "Offbeat History: The Trinity Bay Disaster." *Evening Telegram*, Feb. 26, 1979.

Kitz, Janet F. *Shattered City: The Halifax Explosion.* Halifax: Nimbus, 1989.

Lambert, R. S. *Redcoat Sailor: The Story of Sir Howard Douglas.* Toronto: MacMillan, 1956.

Lord, Walter. *A Night to Remember.* Bantam, 1955.

McKnight, H. A. "The Great Colliery Explosion, 1891." *Amherst Evening Press*, 1891.

Wood, Herbert. *Till We Meet Again: The Sinking of the Empress of Ireland.* Toronto: Image, 1982.

IMAGE SOURCES

Library and Archives Canada: 52, 79, 87, 91, 92, 103, 109 (bottom), 111 (bottom).

Provincial Archives of New Brunswick: 13, 26, 28, 38, 40 (top and bottom), 149.

Nova Scotia Archives and Records Management: 5, 30, 32, 33, 35, 42, 44, 67, 69, 70 (top and bottom), 85, 86, 89, 98, 109 (top), 111 (top), 139, 141 (top and bottom), 142, 144, 146, 154.

Maritime History Archives : xiv, 48, 50 (top and bottom), 53, 55, 57, 60, 73, 76, 94, 96, 102, 105, 107, 129 (bottom), 131, 162, 167.

Centre for Newfoundland Studies: 17, 59, 74.

Fisheries Museum of the Atlantic: 99.

Trinity Historical Society (Newfoundland): 114 (top and bottom), 116.

City of St. John's Archives: 122, 124, 126.

Ena Farrell Edwards: 118, 119, 120 (top and bottom).

Michele Rogers: 178, 182.

Ken Smith: 152.

Cornwallis Museum: 129 (top).

U.S. National Oceanic and Atmospheric Administration (NOAA): 181.

New Brunswick Department of Natural Resources: 11.

Palmer Photography: 36, 169.

Saint John Police Force: 159.

Captain Harry Stone: 164.

INDEX